AF552472

CONSEQUENCES OF DEMOGRAPHIC TRANSITION IN INDIA

CONSEQUENCES OF DEMOGRAPHIC TRANSITION IN INDIA

Edited by
Rajib Lochan Panigrahy

DISCOVERY PUBLISHING HOUSE
NEW DELHI-110002

First Published-2006

ISBN 81-8356-097-0

Published by

DISCOVERY PUBLISHING HOUSE

4831/24, Ansari Road, Prahlad Street,
Darya Ganj, New Delhi-110002 (India)
Phone: 23279245 • Fax: 91-11-23253475
E-mail:dphtemp@indiatimes.com

Printed at:
Arora Enterprises
Laxmi Nagar, Delhi–110 092

Preface

Demography is the picture of population living in a country as its citizen. To a country to build an economy, population is a prerequisite other than its existence on earth with a specific boundary. But, it is a matter of discussion how much it is as compared to the requirement and space for living. With very less population, an economy can not be sound. When population goes beyond the limit, that situation become an alarming danger and the country have to take care of policy measures to reduce it. The beyond limit population growth is better demonstrated in the theory of demographic transition. India and China is in the IIIrd stage of demographic transition. China had ranked in top according to thickly populated country, but in which manner they are reducing their rapid growth of population with strict measures of Policies Research and Development to contribute world economy, that economy is fast growing towards developed economy. By 2020, some economists stated that China may not be the 1st thickly populated country but India will be in that position if the trend of population growth and negligence on economic development will not be checked strictly.

"India a rich country with poor people". It was true and more true in the recent trend of India people on account of its policy measures. India is an agriculturist country. People lives in village i.e. 80 per cent. But, after privatisation liberalisation, globalisation, (PLG) policy followed Indian agriculture retrospects its production, agro-based industries become sick and locked up. Village migrated from rural to urban leaving agriculture. A data of urban population show that in 1951 it was 17 per cent, in 1971 it was 20 per cent, in

1981 it was 23 per cent, in 1991 it was 25 per cent and in 2001 urban population became 27 per cent of the total population lives in India. All the people are fascinating themselves as aristocrats by the influence of fluent mass media live 24 hour T.V. channels, print medias, movies, with sexuality criminal attitude like things, criminal massive news and stories, following of western culture, hatredness of Indian Hindu cultures, beliefs, faiths, scriptures, Purans. The violence of adolescents and youths are increasing day-by-day. Day-by-day jealousy, unbelieveness, telling lies, falsism, juveniles, increasing. Standard of living cannot be maintained with costlier society. Mass unemployment persists the uncertainty among the adults, which reflects in the mind of the adolescents and youths. It pollutes the moral power of the social people due to the rapid population growth to meet the needs of people in the society. Forest depletion, deforestation, soil erosion, less rainfall, disasters, all types of pollutions-soil, water, light, air, sound etc. increases at a galloping rate. These are the causes and affects of mind pollution which creates mental, physical disorder of living people and the new-borns, creates criminal attitudes among them, ecological imbalance, increasing sexual attitudes and make many adolescents track out with love harassment, drug abuses, theft and robbery, even prostitution. A recent data reveals that 10 per cent of hotel girls/prostitutes are from rich and aristocrat families, 30 per cent are from middle class, 45 per cent are from lower class and 15 per cent are from prostitute families. It is a dark figure of sexuality and it shows the image of in what range it is and increasing as epidemics. It is only due to pollution and moral degradation. There is no policy and trends of first track Indian people, officials, political people by which common people can be rectified and followed to make the society rectified. In spite of prospects, virtues in India like country retrospections and evils are increasing day-by-day. For this the Govt. policies and practices of virtues, noble deeds are essential to follow common man.

—Editor

Acknowledgement

At the outset I would like to pour my deep sense of gratitude to my esteemed teacher Dr. S. N. Tripathy, who has been laid the foundation for research writings in books, magazines, conferences, seminars since my college career. Without him this work may not be in this form.

Without the contributors, I may not be an editor. I am very much thankful to them who have made the book up to the mark of publication by recognizing me as its editor. I am very much obliged to person who has helped me by editing scripts and make the book sufficient.

I would like to express my regards to my parent and family members for their encouragement for writing and preparation of the book completed. They also encouraged for writing research topics.

I have to express my gratitude to Mr. Ashok Kumar Jena, Director and Associates of Gayatri Computers for his DTP works and encouragement. Without him the script may not be ready for early publication.

I would owe my deep sense of gratitude to Mr Tilak Wasan Proprietor of Discovery Publications, New Delhi for his kind permission to publish the book. Without his help, it may not see the daylight.

—Editor

List of Contributors

1. **Dr. S.K.Misra** is a Senior Lecture of K.S.U.B. College, Bhanjanagar, Ganjam District of Orissa under Berhampur University.

2. **Dr. Dasarathi Bhuyan** is working as a Lecturer in Political Science in Belaguntha College, Belaguntha under Berhampur Univerity. He is the author of many books and articles. He is a reputed young story writer in Oriya

3. **Mr. Surendra Nath Panda** (M.Sc., B.Ed., L.LM.) is a Senior Advocate of Aska. He is a good writer of socio-economic, legal, science topics. His publications are in reputed journals and newspapers.

4. **Smt. Snehalata Acharya** (MA. B.Ed.) is a Teacher of Biranchi Narayan Girls' High School, Buguda, Ganjam, Orissa.

5. **Mr. Santosh Kumar Pradhan** M.A.(Economics), LL.B. is a lawyer at Aska, good writer on socio-economic topics, attended many conferences and seminars, former Block Coordinator of Hindustan Latex Family Planning Promotion Trust (HLFPPT) sponsored by Ministry of Health and Family Welfare, Government of India at Aska Block. He is a Research Scholar of Berhampur University on Child Labour in Agriculture Sector.

6. **Mr. Laxmi Narayan Panda** (B.Sc., M.Ed.) Science Teacher of Girls' High School, Balimela, Malkanagiri.

7. **Mr Uma Sankar Das** has qualified in MA (Economics), LL.B., PGDRD. He is working as District Project Coordinator for the District of Ganjam, Khurdha, Phulabni and Nayagarh in Health Village Project (sponsored by Govt. of India), HLFPPT.

8. **Balakrishna Padhi** is Master of Economics from Berhampur University and qualified NET examination of UGC.

9. **Premananda Pradhan** is a Research Associate of Major Project under the Chief Project Director Dr. S.N.Tripathy of Aska Science College, Aska.

10. **Mr. Simanchal Maharana**, M.A.(Economics) was a Field Executive of Hindustan Latex Family Planning Promotion Trust & Behavioral Change in Communication sponsored by Ministry of Health and Family Welfare, Government of India under Aska Block and involved with many Social and Research organisations.

11. **Dr. Pradeep Kumar Patnaik** is qualified as MA (Economics), LL.B., Ph.D. working as Head, Dept. of Economics, Khambeya Dora Science College, Pochilima, Hinjilicut, Ganjam, Orissa. He is author of 6 books on economics and 20 articles in reputed journals and edited volumes.

Contents

1

Impediments on the Progress of Tribal Education

Dr. S.K. Misra

A thorough vision into the life of tribes will clear the ghost of conflicts that has taken a wrong portrait in the minds of political bosses and intellectuals who often allege that our "pre-justice against the uplift of the out-castes have almost entirely passed away, and that the difficulties of the problem are negligible". The life, they lead, is quiet separate from urban life and has a little touch to the fruits of democracy. Their difficulties are abundant, their problems are exuberant and the cases of such problems are manifold and steps taken from their removal by governmental authorities are quite disappointing.

The problems of the tribes are innumerable from the historical, anthropological, religious, social, economic, moral, educational, linguistic, health and sanitizing grounds, but attempts have been made to discuss in this research the impediment in spreading education among the tribes .

Educational advancement of tribal children is undoubtedly an important pre-requisite for the welfare and upliftment of the country. Enables it them a better understanding and appreciation of problems so as to adopt a modern and better way of living with full participation in the national plans and programmes for economic, social, political, cultural progress that the nation as whole a making. Amongsts all the schemes for tribal welfare, tribal education should receive topmost priority. With this realization, article 46 of the Constitution of the India provides that government to take special interests to promote the educational economic needs of weaker sections of the people, more particularly of the scheduled castes and scheduled tribes.

It is true that after independence, both government and some voluntary organizations with financial assistance from the government and abroad are trying their best of wipe out illiteracy amongst the backward tribes. But a realistic approach is highly necessary to promote integration in all spheres of tribal education. Spread of education among the tribes deserves serious thought now-a-days. The tribal population in the state of Orissa is 24.06 per cent of the total population and most of them have not yet realised the importance of education.

Many of us feel that they are uncivilized and uncultured but if one comes in contact with them and study them properly with due interest, sympathy, progressive attitude, because of lack of education these innocence and ignorant group of people become the easy victim of socio-economic and political exploitation. Scientific outlook, then certainly, he will opine that these neglected and hated people have advanced in culture. Rather these innocent and ignorant tribes have been economically exploited and eductationally kept backward since long. The basic aim and objective of the government is that the student can attain self-sufficiency by the time he leaves the school if he does not prefer any further education. The state and central governments provide assistance in the form of free distribution of clothes, reading and writing materials and stipends and scholarships. There is reservation for various categories of posts for tribal. In spite of that they are still grouping in darkness of age-old apathy and inertia towards education. The reasons, for those deserve consideration. Some of them are diagnosed by the field officers, administrator and social workers.

Traditional Form of Tribal Education

The traditional form of tribal education prepares a child for the future helps to built up his character through his continuous participation in its day-to-day functioning, by which ideas and thought about social values are formed. By primitive education it is meant that the children are made accustomed with patterns of social set-up convenctional traditional customs by gradual socialization and other approved systematic procedures for imparting such training. As such, a child in future, will born to adjust himself with any situation. Besides, current in all societies, by which the society is continued. The social solidarity thus remains undistributed and as such formal and imformal obligations and duties are automatically observed by an individual through familiar and kinship relations. All these are regarded as informal type of education or learning. As most of the traditional tribal people have no conventional script of their own so their systematic educational pattern is of rigid formalities. Yet, in many primitive people there formal institutations or associations where not only economic pursuits but also rituals, philosophy and political ideas are systematically cultured and propagated to the children to train them up.

Present System of Education

After independence though remarkable changes have occurred in respect of educational patterns of the tribal people, yet these are not considered sufficient to wipeout illiteracy. Educational facilities which are generally extended to the children are of mainly two types:— Traditional and Basic. But, there is no compromise or balance between the two systems and as such basic pattern of education is considered incomplete and somewhat disappointing. But, at present, there are certain handicaps, affecting the spread of education like irregularity in attendance or absentism on the part of their students, due to lack of interest of their guardians to send their boys regularly to schools.

There are so many impediments which may be ameliorated as follows:-

1. It has been observed that poor economic condition of the parents is one of the foremost handicaps in sending their children to the schools. In most cases, the tribal boys have to attend schools without meals for which they are compelled to go out of the school to quench the call their appetite. It is apparent, therefore, that the poor economic

condition of the tribal people stands largely in the way of rapid educational progress because these school-going children help their parents in collecting forest products, firewood, grazing cattle and goats and watching the crops, hunting, fishing and in domestic affairs, Hence, it has been suggested that adequate provision for mid-day meals, supply of dresses, free books and stationary articles may attract more tribal children. The tribal attach considerable importance to their social and religious ceremonies. The working hours and holidays to be observed in the school have to take this into consideration. Any slackness in attendance should not be seriously viewed. So school programme is to be fixed according to festival cycle and agricultural operation of the tribal.

2. Lack of proper encouragement is yet another snag. It is also marked that neighbouring prosperous communities discourage the poor tribal people to avail the educational facilities for their children in order to appoint them in their houses for wages. So, tribal prefer to send their children to the houses of the *Sahukars* instead of sending to the school.

3. Distances of locations of the schools sometimes create hindrances as the boy have to walk many miles to attend these, involving great physical hardship. In such cases opining of more schools in convenient areas, is, therefore a vital requirement for spread of education.

4. Insufficient accommodation in school buildings and lack of equipments etc. are one of the major problems in rural areas. In many areas, there is only a structure without any shutters or flaps for the doors and windows. There is no teaching equipment also. It is also observed that certain schools are running in rented or opened houses which has no such environment for teaching. Some buildings are in a very miserable condition. The buildings should be constructed within the scheduled time with proper surroundings and care must be taken for its yearly repair. Some of the buildings constructed are in dilapidated stage

and can hardly accommodate the students. Hence, repairs and addition construction is highly required with central assistance. Residential schools have well laid gardens and the students work in the garden daily by manuring and irrigating etc. These arrangements for education of the youngsters are not at all attractive or alluring and so they have a general aversion for schools.

5. Selection of right type of teachers with proper qualification is another essential requirements for spread of education in tribal areas. They should be very sympathetic towards the tribal children. They must know the local tribal language to clarify the students about the problems. They should deal with the tribals very carefully showing sentimental affection. The teacher should act as a friend, philosopher and guide to the tribal with a knowledge of their life and culture. He can go to the tribal villages and realise their wants and difficulties and make them understand accordingly. Teachers are pivotal and catalytic agents in the process of transformation of tribal education. They should be trained in orientation centres to study the culture, arts, music, dance, drama etc. of the tribal.

Teachers posted to the primary school in the backward tribal areas are seldom selected on the basis of tribal children. The interior areas are considered as punishment areas due to lack of communication and medical facilities where undesirable persons are being posted who never take any interest. Hence, suitable and well experienced hands may be posted to such areas. They get a vary scanty pay. Hence 20 per cent of their basic pay should be given to primary school teachers as special pay and there should be at least two teachers for smooth running of the institution as well as for the safe-guard of the students. Several Commissions on Tribal Education also suggested that their pay should be raised with residential accommodation. A special cadre is to be created for these type of teachers till these places are well communicated and developed like other developed areas. For primary schools, tribal students after passing from Ashram Schools, are eligible to undergo training. They should not be disturbed except in exceptional cases. The teachers should not be provided with free quarters inside the school campus so that they can raise gardens and demonstrate new variety of crops to the tribes. They should take interest to induce the parents of the tribal students to send their children to the schools.

Medium of Instruction

Mother tongue plays a vital role in the life of individuals. One of the major problems is that of language which is the most controversial aspect which concerns the medium of instruction. Out of 58 languages in the state, 25 belongs to tribal groups. The language has no such script. Moreover to work-out in their own dialect in primary education is difficult as there are innumerable tribal dialects and want of trained teacher. The point is whether the tribes are to be educated in different regional languages from the beginning or the tribal students are to be educated at primary and secondary stages through the medium of their own languages. The greatest need for a scheme like this to be successful, is the adequate number of teachers in tribal languages which is a difficult process. Still then in scheduled areas primary education can be given in their own dialect selecting a few suitable hand from their own community. The Tribal languages are not well equipped to private technical, scientific and advanced education. Again imparting education in tribal languages would incur a huge expenditure which the state can ill-afford. However, there is a considerable thinking that the tribal should be imparted education to infant classes in their own dialects according to "Dhebar Commission".

The subject matter of education for the boys and primary schools specially in tribal concentrated areas should be carefully selected. Local myths, folk songs, dances, human need for food, shelter and clothing, could be included in their textbooks in the regional script so as to enable the tribal to feel that their culture is also seeking equal support by the non-tribal. Since preparation and publication of textbooks in such a large number of tribal dialects are difficult, the maximum that can be done in this line is bringing out primers in certain dialects, written in Oriya script. This will slowly introduced modern and scientific civilization and to facilitate a slow and steady switch over to Oriya medium of instruction. So in order to bring about and fostering and clear understanding, friend spirit, fellow feeling and better appreciation of tribal culture among the field workers, suitable hand-book should be brought out for them by the department without delay. They should not only be trained as teachers but should have aptitude for serving the tribes and respect for their way of life, customs and manners.

Compulsory Primary Education

Compulsory Primary Education is spreading throughout India but for aboriginals, nothing should be imposed on them. Hence speedy arrangements may be made to educate the tribal by supplying mid-day meals, free dresses, reading, and writing materials etc. as regards to primary education, it is seen that a number of school are opened in remotest tribal areas but those are mostly managed by a single teacher. If the teacher remains absent due to some reason, the school is closed. The drawbacks are (1) The tribal students are not interested to attending schools, (2) The atmosphere and the medium of instruction are not congenial to them. The problem of stagnation of tribal students is serious. Most of them do not complete the course they join.

Stagnation affects the general progress of the tribal students in the educational institutions which wastes the investments. Hence, there is necessity for effective co-ordination among the education authority and the teachers to induce tribal parents to send their children to the school.

Administrative Problems

The state Govt. should see that no institution practices in the matter of admission to schools, recruitment of teachers discrimination at any stage on the ground of caste, community or the religion. To end the present system the commission recommended that there should be one system, one policy making body, one operating channel in the tribal areas. Education of aboriginals should be suggested to proper planning and supervision by a board of scholars who have done actual fieldwork. The field workers must have full knowledge and interest in educational methods and practices. They can interpret the culture of the aboriginals in a neat and planned way on their concrete experiences and non-vague sympathy.

Scholarships

The proportion of scholarship where education is still lagging behind will have to be raised. In interiors, where there is no influence of education, number of scholarships may be avoided to that no student will suffer and quit the school. Their scholarship should be paid along with the teacher's monthly pay. At present, out of the stipends 87 per cent goes to converted Christians and advanced tribals. Govt. in consultation of the Planning Commission should prepare a list of the most backward tribals through research institutions and they should be given top most priority for education and other developmental work. Periodical evaluation is to be conducted from time to time by the research bodies and those reports should be taken into consideration in order to know the actual achievements. The State Govt. with the collaboration of the centre, should see that the backward tribals are developed in all respects within the stipulated amount and scheduled time.

Suggestions

It has been observed that to overcome all the difficulties Govt. should give more stress on voluntary organization which work with a missionary spirit and select teachers having requisite qualifications to work amongst the tribals. To wipe out illiteracy a good number of adult education centres should be organised, i.e. the whole tribal education policy should be based on two tyre system, one being adult education both for men and women and the other education of the children. Besides, the mother can be taught the means of maintaining sanitation, health and hygiene so as to influence her children.

Education is the summon bonum of life. It is hardest problem which the educationists and the social scientists have to solve. In the words of Gandhi, "the medium of foreign language through which the higher education has been imparted in India has caused incalculable intellectual and moral injury to the nation. We are too near to our own time to judge the enormity of the damage done". After coming out from schools and colleges our students take no interest to study the language of tribals and thereby understand their difficulties and teach accordingly by which the tribal pupil will undergo no difficulty. Govt. should encourage the students to study. A socialistic society can not be formed by a single person sitting at Delhi throne but by all the persons of the country. Let us join our hands and work in those areas with a new spirit.

REFERENCES

1. *Tribal and Rural Welfare in Orissa*, 1952-53 T.R.W. Publication.
2. *Ground Work of Educational Theory*, James S. Ross.
3. *Tribal Mythes of Orissa*, Verrior Elluin.
4. Anthropology in Tribal Education, *Bulletin of the Cultural Research Institution*, Calcutta, Basu M. N.,1963.
5. Some Suggestion of Tribal Education, *Folklore*, Calcutta Vol. VIII, No.2, Bose N.K.,1966.
6. Report of the Scheduled Area and Scheduled Tribes Commission, New Delhi., Dheder U.N., 1961.
7. *Ways to Educate the Tribal, Adivasi*, Bhowmick P.K.,1967.
8. *A New Deal for Tribal India*, Venier Elwin,1963.

2

Child Labour

A Curse

Surendranath Panda*
Snehalata Acharya**

Introduction

Our children are our future. It was opined by many luminaries. One of them is our former Secretary General of the United Nations Boutros Boutros Ghali. He stated this on the occasion of the third anniversary of the World Summit for Children in September 1993. But the future of the children today is at stake because neither the parents nor the society take care of them adequately. This is a global phenomena. The causes behind it is not only poverty but also lack of common sense of the people at large. So they suffer a lot. Now it is the right time to assess the causes behind the under-development of children. Though we dream of a great future for the children still there are many problems which are not at all possible to overcome individually. So collective efforts are essential to safeguard the rights of a child.

* Advocate, Aska (Orissa).

** Teacher, Biranchi Narayan Girl's High School, Bngda, Orissa.

Problems of the Children

India is a poor country. More than 60 per cent of its population are below poverty line. They do not even get two square meals in a day. But on the other hand it is a populace country. According to the recent census it is second in the world. The first position in population goes to Chine. Poverty in one side and population in the other side are playing their role to put the children in a very difficult condition. Most of the children under the age group of 5 to 14 are illiterate. They suffer from malnutrition and slavery. Minor girls are also forced to prostitution which is the most hazardous position of a child. It has been reported in 1983 that one crore seventy four children are working as labourers. Out of them 90 per cent belongs to the villages. They get a meagre amount though they work for 10 to 12 hours per day. They get 50 per cent less wages for the same work done by an adult labourer.

It has also been reported that children in the age group of 3 to 15 are working as labourers in match factories, cracker factories where they come in contact with very poisonous chemicals resulting hazardous health condition. A major section of the children are also working in Bidi manufacturing units round the clock resulting health problems like Asthma and Tuberculosis. Now-a-day child labour is rampant in our society. Most of the children are working as labourers in the cracker factories of Sivakasi in Tamilnadu. Nearly more than 2 crores of children are working in weaving of carpets. Nearly more than 2 crores of children are working in different tea stalls, hotels, agriculture farms, small cottage industries in different parts of the country. They are not well nursed by the proprietors of the units. Most of the children are also engaged as domestic labourers. Their role is to take care of the houses of their boss. They wash the utensils, broom the house, water the garden and they take care of the child of the house owner only for two square meals.

Role of Children in Nation Building

The future of the nation depends on its individuals. So the individual should have moral character with a religious bend of mind. Then only he will guide the child to be a full-fledged man. Literary play an important role to build the nation. Each and every parent should take care of his child to make him literate. Unless the child knows what is what he can not distinguish between right and wrong in later stage of his life. The role of a child in nation-building is very vital. Proper environment should be afforded to him. Love, affection, team spirit should be inculcated with child. Parents must play not only as an individual but also as a guide, friend, philosopher for his child. Unless the child is good and religious he will not think of a bright society. We must have pollution free society. Not only the air pollution or noise pollution but also pollution of character should be checked at the initial stage of a child. Then only the future of the globe will be bright.

Right of a Child

Our Constitution guarantees the safety of a child. We derive power from the Constitution. Article 24 of the Constitution deals with child labour. There is a restriction as per Article 24 of the Indian Constitution that no child below the age group of 14 will be allowed to work as a labourer in any industry or mines where the life is at danger. Similar provisions are contemplated in Industries Act, Mines Act. But these provisions are not applied practically because of the bondage of poverty, illiteracy and lack of common sense.

On 20th November 1989 a convention on Rights of Child was held. That was the first International Legal Instrument which laid down guarantee for the Child's Human Rights. 61 countries signed the Convention on 26th January 1990, the first day it was opened for the signature. The Convention entered into force against economic exploitation and social neglect. In early days the rights of the children were guided by certain measures. In that regard the League of Nations adopted in 1924 the General declaration. In a later stage the treaty of law to children's rights became evident. International year of the child was observed in 1979. But practically we have problems for the children.

The Fundamental Rights of the children are invaded. They are tortured and forced to be child labourers instead of playing, laughing and prosecuting studies. They work in farms, mines, restaurants, factories as servants. Poverty and illiteracy are two major factors which force them to be child labours. So consciousness of parents as well as the society will play a vital role to free them from the bondage of child labour.

Different Volunteer Organisations/NGOs play a major role to guide them to have a better life. But because of ignorance of the people they have not achieved their target. Birth control will be an important factor to check the child labour. Unless birth control is done prudently then the economic condition and social obligation will be at stake resulting crimes in the society. So we should start work to have a child labour free country not only enacting different legislatious but by creating awarness among the people. Then only we will have a child labour free country and the dreams of our forefathers will become fruitful.

Child labour should be discouraged in each and every angle and collective efforts should be made for the education, cloth and health of every child. Then only the curse of child labour can be lifted.

REFERENCES

1. Basu, D.D.—*Constitution Law of India,* 8th Edition, Prentice Hall of India, 1991.
2. Kashyap, S.C.—*Our constitution—An Introduction to India & Constitution Law*, 2nd Edition, National Book Trust, India, 1995.
3. Punit Kumar—*Rights of Child, Employment News,* Dated 12-8 Nov' 1994.
4. Rath, Dr. Nirupam—Child Labour & Its Safety ("Sisu Sramika O Tara Nirapatta" in Oriya), *The Samaj*, Oriya Daily, 1994.
5. Sen, Maitree—*The Curse of Child Labour*, Vibes (Indian Express) Dated 6.2.2002.
6. Kar, Souribandhu—Labour & Its Life in Footpath ("Sramika O Rasthare Banchuthiba Tara Jeevan" in Oriya), *The Anupam Bharat*, Oriya Daily dated 05th Feb' 2002.
7. Bangia, R.K.—*Indian Contract Act*, 8th Edition, Allahabad Law Agency, 1999.
8. Chander, Dr. Prakash—*India Govt. & Politics*, Book Hive, New Delhi 1984.
9. *Company Law* (Question-Answer), Asish Law Agency, Berhampur, Orissa.
10. Fitzgerald, P.J.—*Salmond on Jurisprudence*, 12th Edition, Sweet & Maxwell, London, 1988.
11. Pandey, J.N.—*Constitutional Law of India*, 27th Edition, Central Law Agency, Allahabad, 1994.

3

Backward Classes and Social Change

Dr. Dasarathi Bhuyan

Two-thirds or more of the population of India are very backward, being illiterate and living in utter poverty. There are three broad divisions among the backward classes: (a) The Scheduled Castes (Harijans), (b) Scheduled Tribes (Garijans) and (c) The Other Backward Class. The SC and ST are listed in the constitution while the other backward class is unlisted and loosely defined; it is the least homogeneous. As a result, the problem of other backward classes is very complicated and very difficult to deal with. While it is possible to have an all India list of SC on the basis of untouchability and the scheduled tribes on the basis of their way of life, it is impossible to have any such list for the Other Backward Class.

The Position of Scheduled Castes

One of the earliest references to this group appears in the *Chandogya Upanishad* which uses the term "Chandala". The term referred to a degraded person who is ranked along with the dog and the pig. Buddhist Jatakas of the second century B.C, also speak of the Chandalas as a despised group living outside the village, who speak a special dialect and have their own hereditary occupation. The *Dharma-sastras* declare the Chandala to be the progeny of a Brahmin women and a Sudra man. Manu also declared that these People lived out side the village and that they were prohibited from entering the villages and towns in the day time. These statements are confirmed by the observations of Alberuni, who wrote in about 1020 A.D. He noted the Dom and the Chandala as the two groups who did the dirty work like cleaning the village and who were distinguished by their occupations.

But it is very difficult to imagine that persons born out of forbidden sex contacts were numerous enough to form a separate caste group, since they are to be found practically in all the villages of India. It is possible that because they were following occupations, which were despised, they were characterized by the *Dharmasastras* as equivalent to the despicable progeny of forbidden sex relations. As G.S. Ghurye in his book "Caste, Class and Occupation", writes, "Ideas of purity, whether occupational or ceremonial, which are found to have been a factor in the genesis of caste are the very soul of the idea and practice of untouchability". Thus, because they were following occupations like scavenging, doing leather work, removing dead cattle from the village, and so on, they were looked upon as a profane group, contact with whom was defiling. So they were required to live in a separate colony out side the village.

The practice of untouchability was at its worst in different parts of the Kerala state in the south-west corner of the country. As A. Aiyappan writes, "while the belief in human beings as carriers of graded degrees of ritual impurity is common to all Hindus, these manifestations are nowhere as hypertrophied as in Kerala. To avoid upper castes being polluted, the distance at which the polluting castes have to remain has been fixed and prescribed by tradition." Among the untouchables also there are various castes; the distance at which these castes had to remain, varied from about 30 feet to about 150 feet. According to Ambedkar, these groups Persisted in Practising Buddhism even after the bulk of the Hindus gave it up and so they were banished from the villages. This view also appears to be rather far fetched.

In the opinion of B. Kupuswamy, "It looks as if these groups of people were declared untouchable and were made to live outside the villages for two reasons. First, they were following the lowest kinds of occupations like scavenging, leatherwork, removal of the carrion, etc; and second, they persisted in eating beef, which was condemned as the most heinous crime by the caste Hindus. As Srinivas notes, "They are an integral part of the village life, they perform certain essential tasks in agriculture, they are often village servants, messengers and sweepers, and they beat the drum at village festivals and remove the leaves on which people have dined at community dinners".

The Position of Scheduled Tribes

Seven per cent of the total populations are leading the tribal way of life. According to the scheduled tribe lists, modification order 1956 there are 414 different tribes in the various states in India. In respect of scheduled tribes Chhatisgarh, Jharkhand, Orissa have the largest population.

One of the chief difficulties is the problem of definition. The Government of India have taken the simple step of listing the tribes and have called them the Scheduled Tribes. A tribe is an indigenous homogenous unit speaking a common language, claiming a common descent, living in a particular geographic area, backward in technology, preliterate, loyally observing social and political customs based on kinship".

The economic status of the tribes vary all the way from poor food gathers to agriculturists, plantation labour, and industrial labour. The kadars; the Malapantaram, the Paniyans of Kerala, the paliyan of Tamil Nadu, the Kudukurubas of Mysore are dependent on forest products. They are essentially food gathers. They collect fruits, edible roots and honey from the forest and supplement these with hunting or chase of animals. Where there are ponds and rivers they catch fish.

The bulk of the tribal population of India depends on some form of agriculture with forest produce as secondary support. The Oraon, the Munda, the Bhill, the santhal, the Majhwar, the Kharwar, the Baiga, the Korwa, the Gond and the Ho practice shifting axe cultivation consisting of feeling the trees on a hillside a little before the monsoon and setting them on fire. When the earth is covered over by a layer of ashes and when the rains fall, they scatter seeds and with an occasional shower of rain the seeds take root and grow. But the crops are scarce and are of an inferior quality. The soil becomes impoverished in the absence of ploughing and manuring. So they sift to another valley and cut the trees there. This process of agriculture besides being inadequate, is very wasteful as it leads to deforestation and soil erosion and floods. So the forest laws prevent shifting cultivation. This leads to terrible hardship to the tribal people. Further, land alienation is the most important problem affecting these groups.

Many of the tribes are good at handicrafts which include basket mating, spinning and weaving. There are some functional classes among the Saore, the Kond, and the Gond who devote themselves to metal working, cane working, pottery, weaving and so on. The Tribal people of northeastern states have an economy midway between the food gathering and primitive agriculture. Their social and economic organizations are built around their cattle, which form the economic, as well as the religions basis of the life of the tribe.

Other Backward Classes

The backward Class movement started in the early part of the twentieth century, when schools and colleges were giving courses in secular subjects through the medium of English, only the castes and classes with the tradition of education utilized the opportunity to educate themselves. As a result only the members of these castes and classes could get the jobs in the Government services and increase their prestige. This further increased the cultural, social and economic distance between them and the lower castes. This made the lower castes to realize that they were nowhere in this situation. They wanted a share in the new opportunities. As Srinivas himself puts it, the lower castes realized that mere Sanskritization was not enough. It did not provide them the avenue for social mobility and obtain well-paid and prestigious jobs in the administrative services. So they desired to get themselves educated through the English medium in order to qualify themselves for the new jobs in the administration and new profession like law, mediciene, engineering etc. Srinivas further says, "It is no accident that the movement was strongest in peninsular India, where only one caste, the Brahamins enjoyed and preponderance in higher education, the professions and Government employment. It is also the area where a wide social and cultural gulf obtained between the Brahmins and others".

However, it was soon realized that the qualified youth could not get admission in the professional courses and the postgraduate courses because admission was based on marks in the High School and college examinations. Here they were at a handicap since the boys form the homes with education as a tradition were able to secure high marks. Another complication arose as a result of the fact that the teachers and examiners were from the forward castes. This gave rise to the fear that they were being discriminated on the basis of caste. A similar situation arose when they competed for jobs in the Government services. Here also the appointing authorities at the lower levels were mostly Brahmins. With not very high marks and with the prevalence of nepotism, the young men from the lower castes found themselves at a disadvantage. This led to anti-Brahmin feelings both among the leaders of various lower castes and the frustrated youth. Thus the aim of the backward class movement at this stage was to limit the Brahmin monopoly in the two fields of education and appointment to Government posts. As Srinivas writes, "The opposition to Brahmin dominance did not come from the low and the oppressed castes but from the leaders of the powerful, rural dominant castes such as the Kammas and Raddis of the Telugu country, the Vellalas of the Tamilnadu and the Nayar of Kerala." These were high caste groups with a social position next to the Brahmins. They included not only the Hindus but also the Muslims, Christians and other Communities. This is the important reason why the term used to describe these groups is "Backward classes" and not "Backward castes".

Experience in the last quarter of a century has clearly shown that the number of groups in the list increases rather than decreases with the time. Concessions create a vested interest in backwardness. No group wants to forego the concession; it is because no group as a whole can truly say that all its members have now become 'forward' that no section of the group needs special concessions. It is true that, when the leaders of these groups put forward the case in the parliament, their arguments are neither untrue nor unjust.

The Backward Class Commission was appointed in 1953 with Kaka Kalekar as the Chairman. The commission was appointed according to the Article 340 of the Constitution. The Commission was asked to determine the criteria to be adopted to provide concessions to "Socially and educationally backward classes" besides the Scheduled Castes and Scheduled Tribes. The Commission was also asked to prepare a list of such classes. Inaugurating the Commission, the late prime minister Nehru said that he disliked the term "backward classes" since ninety per cent of the people were poor and backward.

One of the first recommendations of the Commission was that the 1961 census should provide caste wise figures so that "before the disease of caste is destroyed all facts about it have to be noted and classified in a scientific manner as in a clinical record". The commission also recommended that certain sections of the Muslims, Christians, Sikhs should be included among the other "Backward Classes".

As regards causes for backwardness, the Commission has concluded "A" variety of causes— social, environmental, economic and political—have operated both openly and in a subtle form for centuries to create the present colossal problem of backwardness. Economic backwardness is the result and not the cause of many social evils".

With respect to criteria of backwardness the Commission recommended for general guidance:

1. Low social position in the traditional caste hierarchy.
2. Lack of education in the major section of the caste or community.
3. Inadequate or no representation in government service.
4. Inadequate representation in the field or trade, commerce and industry.

Social Change among Them

One significant features in the twentieth century has been the weakening of the barriers between the sub-caste and the barriers arising out of pollution. Higher education, Government employment, and urbanization have led to the crumbling of the sub-caste barriers. The endogamous circle widened and educated people tended to look upon the barriers of the sub-caste as not insurmountable when it came to finding suitable brides and bridegrooms for their children. This was also due to the new movement of All-India caste conferences, which fought for the consolidation of caste in the country as a whole and the breaking down of the sub-caste barriers. It may be mentioned that the caste system, as it was practiced, restricted the choice of marriage not only to the caste and the sub-caste but also to the sub-caste within the linguistic zone and even there practically within the district or the neighbouring districts. The All-India caste conferences worked against these regional, linguistic and sub-caste barriers. A third-movement responsible for the weakening of the barriers was the nationalist movement which launched mass campaign under the leadership of Mahatma Gandhi. His campaign against untouchability lead to the weakening of the notions of pollution.

Some of the tribal people like Santhals, the Kond and the Gond from Bihar, Chattisgarh, Jharkhand, Orissa and Madhya Pradesh have migrated in large numbers to Assam and work on the plantations. The areas in Jharkhand, Chattishgarh, Orissa, Madhya Pradesh, and West Bengal, which are rich in coal, iron, etc, have led to the emergence of industrial labour. It is estimated that about half of the labourers in the manganese industry of Madhya Pradesh are tribal people. The Santhal and the Ho are prominent in the Bihar iron industry. Nearly the entire unskilled labour force of the Tata Iron and Steel Co are tribals. There is both the inside "push" following economic hardship due to land alienation, indebtedness and out side pull due to demand for labour in tea plantations and in industries. Thus, the tribesmen have been transplanted from the tribal life to the urban life and so are confronted by great difficulties in social adjustment.

As D.N. Majumdar puts it "Today most of these tribes have come in contact with advanced communities, have learnt traits of their neighbours, have borrowed patterns of their dress and developed an intricate material economy. Some of these tribes have progressed at a tremendous pace effecting in a few years changes which have taken centuries to achieve in other areas".

These contacts have arisen, in a number of ways. First, the itinerant vendors from the neighboring villages and towns who have taken clothes and trinkets, metal utensils, patent medicines to the hills and the Jungles. Second there are administrative officers who have gone into these areas because of the forest laws and revenue laws. Third, there were Christian Missionaries who wanted to convert them to Christianity in order to save their souls. Forthy , all types of contact have been greatly increased because of the tremendous developments in transport and communication. Finally, the existence of mineral resources in and around primitive tracts have led to the establishment of mines, industries, and educational institutions.

As a result of these cultural contacts, there have been changes, in their food habits, dress, ways of living etc. and the various tribes of India are now living at different cultural levels. Some of these tribal groups however, continue to line even now in seclusion, comparatively uninfluenced by these cultural contacts. But some of the groups have adopted the Hindu customs because of their association with the village people. Others have been converted to Christianity. But the large majority of the tribal groups in India have now more or less settled down in the rural areas taking to agricultural and other allied occupation.

However, there was a school of thought, which favoured isolation. Another school particularly advocated by the social reformers and voluntary organisations, was one for assimilation of these tribal groups either into Christianity and Hinduism. The Christian missionaries and some social reformers like Thakkar Bapa have recommended this. The third view, which is actively followed in the recent years; is that of integration. The policy of integration aims at developing a creative adjustment between tribes and non-tribes of India leading to responsible partnership.

In conclusion, it may be pointed out that a big social change has come among the Harijans (SC) and to Girijans (ST) on the basis of the temple entry legislation, the reservation of seats in Parliament and the state legislatures, the provision of educational facilities and employment opportunities. During the last fifty years, thousand of SC & ST families have moved from the lowest class to the middle class. Thousands of them have been members of the legislature in the state and central parliament, some persons chief ministers and President of India etc,. Further, as it has been noticed earlier, the Government has taken caste as the basis for the upliftment programme.

On the other hand, the practice of untouchability is in its virulent form in the villages where 80 per cent of the population live. Caste is the most important dimension in the social structure of the village and the members of the Harijan castes are too few in the village to fight for their rights and too divided among themselves to consolidate their limited strength to fight for their rights. Thus the one big change in the position of the Harijans (SC) is that in the urban areas on the basis of their education, employment and income, they are in a position to move into the middle class, but in the villages it is impossible for them to experience any change in status.

REFERENCES

1. Ayyappan, A.,—*Social Revolution in a Kerala Village*, Asia Publishing House, Bombay, 1965.
2. Chattopadhyaya, S. — *Social Life in Ancient India*, Academic Publishers, Calcutta, 1965.
3. Ghurye, G.S. — *Caste, Class and Occupation*, Popular Prakashan, Bombay, 1961.
4. Gandhi, M.K. — *Autobiography*, Navajeevan Press, Ahmedabad, 1940.
5. Kupuswamy, B., — *Social Change in India*, Vikas Publishing House, Ghaziabad.
6. Nayer, V.K.S. — Communal Interest Groups in Kerala, In Smith's ed., *South Asian Politics and Religion*, Princeton, 1966.
7. Srinivas, M.N. — *Social Change in Modern India*, Allied Publications, Bombay, 1966.

4

Education and Training for HRD in India

Rajib Lochan Panigrahy*

Abstract

This chapter contains the descriptions about how our Indian Human Resources are developed and under threat. HRD is essential for the development of an economy and industrial concern. HRD can be attained by education and training which accelerate the economic development and productivity.

HRD in Indian Economy—At a Glance

"Our Principal Asset is Our People"

HRD is the development as sustainable process of expanding the capabilities of people and of which seeks to mobilize human resources primarily health, education, skill development through different training programmes and allied services, that should be the central elements of such a development strategy.

HRD is not only essential to the individuals of an organisation but also in general public of an economy. So, that the industry or

* Swami Sivananda Polytechnic, (Under Berhampur University, Orissa), Aska, Ganjam (Orissa) — 761 110.

economy will be developed. The essential ingredient of social or industry policy concerning labour and employment has been to treat labour not only as resources for development but as a partner and beneficiary of social and economic development. The administrators and bureaucrats have to keep in mind for an economy like other factors of production that labour is the essential input for production. So, the production function is

$$Q = (K, L, E, M)$$

Here, K is capital,

L is labour

E is energy and fuel

M is material

Many of the legislative provisions protecting labour in various sectors strengthened including social security measures made comprehensive to include various kinds of risks. When the industrial disputes where enacted the mechanism for fixing and implementing minimum wages was developed by Minimum Wages Act,1948 for the economy as a whole in industrial concerns.

The basic facilities behind all the economic and legislative measures to develop the quality of human resources with timely and fair wage payment as decided by Govt. from time to time and other benefits to be availed by person concerned like security of life and property, education, health etc. considering social justice and protecting human rights for promoting an appropriate productive climate.

The Minimum Wages Act, 1948 not only meant for providing minimum wages to the labourers of an industry, but also to provide minimum wages in general throughout India and Central and State level. Due to non-payment of minimum wages, the people of Bihar, U.P, M.P, and Orissa are generally migrating to other states/regions. Due to such migration they are facing the problems of health-hazard even HIV/AIDS. There are sufficient data to reveal. India has rich natural resources. Most of people depending on agriculture. So on agricultural products are easily available as input to industry which can create healthy economy. In spite of building up agro-industries, the industries becoming sick and also closing day-by-day. How a measurable condition of our human resources. Even in India people die in starvation. 40 per cent of Indians are below poverty line and illiterate.

Data reveals that the Indian human resources are developed because the people serving abroad are rich resources, if they will be found in India, they are less important. The quality of Indian human resources is as data shows (as on) July 2000.

3.22 million American population, 38 per cent Doctors in America, 12 per cent Scientists in America, 36 per cent of NASA employees, 34 per cent IBM employees, 17 per cent INTEL employees, 13 per cent XEROX employees are Indian.

**Herald Sun* said— "Telesta (an Australian electronic company) is using Indian computer workers on sweat shop wages to replace high paid Australians. The telecom giant which remains 50.1 per cent owned by Australian tax payers has almost 100 Indian programmers and analysts". *Herald Sun* also reported the media that even starting salary in India is higher than the Rs.3.5 lakh per year (1 Australian Dollar = Rs. 29.07).

And the history reveals, Indian invented the number system, zero (by Aryabhatta), largest number tera (10^{12}) pi, algebra, trigonometry, calculus navigation , astronomy, chess (sataranga). Indian had the first university Takshila and first language Sanskrit. So, scientists found Pout that Sanskrit is the only language suitable for computer data transformation system.

The richest person of the world the Chairman of MS company of USA strongly remarked that Indian people are not only sincere, obedient, hardworking but intelligent, responsible and rich in mathematics. But, there is a big questions here, how Indian human resources is not developed. If they are developed, so the country should be developed one. Hence, the demand arises from different levels the HRD policies should design and redesign continuously with the potential human resources, so that the labour will be productive factors for development.

Thus, education and training for individuals and organisations is of paramount importance to intensive and absorb new and complex technological needs because the rapid technological change occurs everyday. The vocational and technical education forms the core of the formal education system. With this there is a requirement of higher level of cognitive skills and knowledge say R&D activities and still higher level of education and research.

In India the Minimum Wages Act passed in 1948 followed by the Equal Remuneration Act, 1976 obtaining minimum wages or equal wages is still a far cry generally in unorganised sector and in many organized sector also with several plea.

Kerala is an exemplary of full literacy and education. Promoting education in society is an important pre-condition for attaining HRD. It is still only one of its essential dimensions. Health and sanitation is the other important dimension of HRD. Lack of sound health, education, literacy, sanitation, nutrious food, consciousness about rapid population growth, etc. the Indian human resources are lagging behind which reflects on the economy as a whole and organisation concerned. In Kerala due to its education promotion, the rate of infant mortality reduced to below 20 per 1000 childbirth, which is very favourable in comparison to the developed countries of western Europe. In comparison to India's population growth, Kerala remains very stable growth, so its human resources are developed.

Now the very important question arises—what is our object? Raising our capacity to produces more goods and services with excessive reliance on foreign aid and to raise standard of living, where the people are under the condition of extreme deprivation and poverty. But, raising productivity in the country which ultimately should reach the people at the bottom level of the social ladder who do not have the purchasing power to secure their legitimate share of such goods and services. It is therefore essential to be concerned with not merely the generation of income but also its distribution.

In spite of all these, due to defective policy measures, Kerala face unemployment, high cost of living, etc. which hinders HRD in Kerala. one evidence of under-employment is that there are 364 constables in Kerala, out of which 30 are undergraduates, 294 are graduates, 24 are postgraduates, 16 are Law graduate out of which 6 have Advocacy. Here one questions arises where is HRD in Kerala?

After more than half of the century of India's independence, it is under-developed with 2nd highest populated country, Delhi being the Capital of India is the 4th polluted cities in the globe. India is 2nd HIV/AIDS affected nation in the world and highest in ASIA.

In this consequence, it will be extremely useful to examine education and training system in the context of equipping future manpower with requisite job-oriented skill and expertise.

HRD at Industrial Context

The social and economic development of a state is only possible when the people and the state realize and perform the responsibilities in the befitting manner. In order to perform the responsibilities in a most befitting manner, men management is essential.

The **M**s are— **M**an, **M**achine, **M**aterial, **M**oney and **M**arket are the basic factors for management of an organisation and economy. Thus a separate scientific systematic department—Human Resource Development (HRD) evaluated in almost all industries. The effective functioning of every business organisation depends not only on available material and financial resources but how one pool the ability, efficiency and willingness of human resources to work.

So, A.P. Soloan remarked that— "No organisation is sounder than its men".

HRD at industries always aims at industrial development, the growth of the organisation by increasing productivity and for the wholesome division of the personality of the industrial worker. Due to importance of Human Resources and its complexity on over changing psychology, behaviour and attitude of persons at work, the management functions for HRD viz. planning, organizing, coordinating, directing, controlling, selecting for placement of right man in the right place to achieve the organizational goal. Thus, the HRD can be done by giving the opportunity to the workers for participation in decision-making at the top level providing proper training and education to different types of personnel according to the requirement.

Model

Education is the tool of increasing technical skill of a work, which ultimately increases productivity. It has taken the entering date of an worker —v, time —t. The average productivity of a representative worker in an age group is:

$p(v, t) = e^{gt} [a(v) + b(v)\, m(v, t)];\ m(v, t) > 0$............$1^{st}$ eq^n

g is the rate of technical progress exogenous.

$e^{gt} a(v)$ is the exogenous component of productivity.

$m(v, t)$ is the level of qualification of standard worker which depends on the factors appearing in the right hand side of the following eq^n.

$M(v, t) = e^{-k(v)t} u(v, t) - h(v)\, m(v, t)$ ....2nd eq^n

$K(v) > 0$ is the known coefficient, which depends on the workers resistance to absorbing new knowledge. It implies that pure learning capacity decrease overtime after a certain age. It is found from first eq^n. Due to education, g increase and ultimately productivity.

BLOCK DIAGRAM

The flowing Block Diagram illustrates how education and training promotes HRD

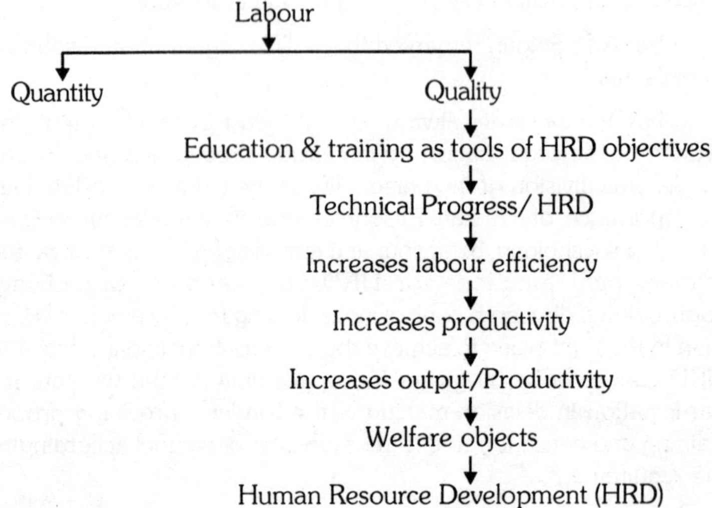

It reveals that the productivity gain is the harbinger of the developed economy and industrial concern, which can be attained by qualitative improvement of labour. Education and training are the tools for improving the quality of human resources; ultimately attain HRD offering welfare objects.

REFERENCES

1. Rajib Lochan Panigrahy — *Human Resource Development and Labour Welfare* (2002), Common Wealth Publishers, New Delhi.
2. Balasahib Vikhe Patil — Indian Reforms & HRD, *Indian Journal of Economics* (pp. 19 to 24), January-March' 2000.
3. Meera Allen & S.N. Misra — Structural Reforms and Employment Issues, *Indian Journal of Economics* (pp. 271 to 292), April-July' 2001.
4. V. Nirmala et al. — Genderwise Minimum Wages, Wage Differentials and Determinants — A Micro Analysis of Agricultural Labourers, *Indian Journal of Economics*, April-July' 2001.
5. Alberto Quadrio — Planning Manpower, Education & Economic Growth, *Human Resource Employment & Development*, Vol. 3 (1998) Edited by Weisbred & Helen Hughs.
6. Alain Minget & J.C. Eicher — The Higher Education and Employment Markets in France, *HR Employment & Development*, Vol. 3 (1983) Edited by Burton Weisbred & Helen Hughs.
7. *Interesting Facts About India & Indians* (p. 10) — East and West, July, 2000.
8. Punita Jasrotia — The Need of Human Resource Accounting, IT People Supplement of Express Computer Weekly (December 6, 2001).
9. Prof. Jayashree Roy of Jadavpur University, Calcutta — Theoretical and Statistical Models (Chapter 2) of Demand for Energy in Indian Industries.
10. Rajib Lochan Panigrahy — Market Process of Computer Science & Applications, *The Journal of Commerce & Economics* (2000), Berhampur, Orissa.
11. *Y. Yatish Rajwat — Aussie are Now Crying Foul Over the Desi IT Pros, Telstra Hired 100 Indian Engineers At Low Wages, *The Economic Times* Dated 25.4.2003.

5

Alternative Path to Demographic Transition

Uma Sankar Das

There is today a pressing need for limiting the family size at a personal level and for the control of population at a national level. This importance of birth control at a personal level has arisen through increased cost of living, scarcity of accommodation, a desire for better education for children in the present competitive world, and an overall desire for an improved standard of living.

The population in India has been growing rapidly. It has doubled in India from 344 million in 1947 to 685 million in 1981 and is likely to double in the next 30 years. The social-economic problems of overpopulation are too well known to be discussed here. Health and medical grounds are the other considerations for birth control. It is reckoned that a woman below 20 years is not generally physically grown to produce a child. If she does produce, she becomes a high-risk case during pregnancy and labour, and is likely to deliver a low birth weight newborn. Spacing birth control is thus; seen as a health measure. A multifarious woman from low income group generally suffers from malnutrition and is predisposed to prolapsed, stress in continence, chronic cervicitis and cancer of the cervix. The spacing of childbirth and limiting the number of pregnancies are strongly desirable in such cases, as also in a patient with a heart disease. A history of two Caesarean sections is indicative of a repeat Caesarean section in subsequent pregnancy, which exposes the patient to grave gynaecological problems. In India, it is customary to offer sterilization operation at the time of third Caesarean section, and sometimes during second caesarean section. Other cases needing sterilization includes the mentally retarded women and those suffering from serious psychiatric disorder like schizophrenia. A woman who has borne a child with a genetic disorder needs genetic counselling and may have to be advised against future pregnancy.

It would appear that in one sense we have a broad choice between two historical paths to success in achieving population stabilization goals—and indeed we have to combine elements of both. First there is the East Asian path to demographic transition—through state led public action for social development securing large behaviour changes in favour of low fertility low mortality with low social breakdown. Of course the extent to which such behaviour changes were voluntary would depend on the content of democratic freedoms in each country. Second there is the post-modern Western path which has also completed the transition but within a far-reaching social security system. This model has also enabled low fertility and low mortality but has been accompanied in many cases with substantial social costs in high teen-age pregnancy, high divorce and out of wedlock children. What is common to both paths is the sustained positive role of the State in political commitment, a caring approach and sustained long term allocation of resources to social development. This has facilitated both public action and evolution of partnerships. This has provided greater choices among contraceptive services, and encouraged multiple channels of delivery for more information about services and how to access them. Clearly our choice must lie closer to the former path but moderated by our democratic constitutional and social cultural context. Unmet needs must therefore be attended to keeping in mind our pluralistic society and regional diversities and dynamic changes in new methods of contraception. In our view this would call for a three-fold approach within which interventions could be identified at various levels for better implementation of family welfare services, of which unmet need forms a part.

First: *Strengthen existing strategies and sharpen the focus of existing infrastructure for delivery of quality service. In the near term public health infrastructure will have to bear the brunt of the effort, given the scale of the problem.*

States must streamline their planning, resource mobilizing and coordinating tasks under ongoing contraception programs to obtain better value for resources deployed. Program implementation must be steadily improved in the States with focussed effort without being too defensive about some failures in the past

Second: *To expand the basket of choices for contraceptives taking into account the variety of new demands arising from latent and manifest changes among social classes and across regions and to improve easy availability of wider choice through more channels for distribution.*

The wider range in contraceptives will be chosen from among those new spacing and long acting products which have been technologically validated in Indian conditions and found locally acceptable. Such an expansion of choice must cover both rural and urban needs and cut across socio-economic classes at different levels of awareness, wherever possible through a community based outreach and coverage.

For distribution of subsidized sales, selected private and non-governmental agencies can be assigned to do social marketing subject to guidelines. Social marketing will augment commercially distributed products and government provided services but it should also be relevant to local needs and practices and must ensure minimum outcomes and value for money spent on subsidy.

Last: *We must link family planning services to new opportunities arising from decentralization and economic reforms such as health insurance, concern for human rights and the statutory right to information and link with panchayats to assign practical tasks to monitor quality and accountability and locate population control tasks within a quality of life framework as was suggested by the Swaminathan Committee.*

It is difficult to establish any direct co-relation between contraceptive prevalence, levels of public expenditure and crude birth rates. There are many intermediate factors within and outside the demographic and health sectors that influence such relationships. Wherever social development had been a sustained concern and become a politically salient issue there has been improvement in the easy availability, wider choice, more channels for distribution and increased contraceptive prevalence. On many fronts there has been progress.

There is today a pressing need for limiting the family size at a personal level and for the control of population at a national level. This importance of birth control at a personal level has arisen through increased cost of living, scarcity of accommodation, a desire for better education for children in the present competitive world, and an overall desire for an improved standard of living.

What is Contraceptive

A method or a system, which allows intercourse and yet prevents conception is called contraceptive method. This contraception may be temporary when the effect of preventing pregnancy lasts while the couple uses the method but the fertility returns immediately or within a few months of its discontinuation. The permanent contraceptive methods are surgical: tubectomy in a women and vasectomy in a man.

Methods of Contraception

1. Natural Methods:
   - (a) Abstinence during the fertile phase
   - (b) Withdrawal (coitus interrupts)
2. Barrier contraceptives:
   - (a) Use of condoms by male
   - (b) Use of spermicidal agents
   - (c) Douching
   - (d) Use of diaphragm in the vagina and cervix
   - (e) Use of hormones which after alter the cervical mucus and prevent entry of sperms in to the cervical canals
3. Intrauterine contraceptive devices (IUD)

4. Suppression of spermatogenesis
5. Suppression of ovulation with hormones-hormonal contraceptives
6. Interceptive agents (post-coital contraception)
7. Immunological method
8. Surgical sterilization

Emergency Contraception Facility

It is noted that as recommended by the National Consortium on Emergency Contraception the use of the "morning after" pill in the country is being tested by the ICMR through operations research projects with the collaboration of 12 medical colleges in different parts of the country. The results are awaited. Parivar Sewa Sansthan too has brought out its own morning after pill, called No Preg, and has sought a no objection from the Drug Controller of India for social marketing of this pill. It was also noted that Use of IUDs can also be used as an emergency contraception. During 2000, the Population Council completed a media campaign on emergency contraception a manual on emergency contraception has been widely disseminated to users, service providers, and policy-makers in India, and has now been adapted for use in Bangladesh. Efforts are continuing to make abortions safe in the country. The subgroup was informed that following a recent National Conference several recommendations intended to make early abortions safe and accessible are being reviewed. Including an amendment devolving powers of approval of the premises and the provider for carrying out medical termination of pregnancy to the district level, instead of the earlier state level.

Table 5.1: Prevention and management of unwanted pregnancy method-wise performance during last four years (from 1996-97 to 1999-2000)

Method	*1996-97*	*1997-98*	*1998-99*	*1999-2000*
Sterilization	3870226	4238514	4181951	4438961
IUDs	5680671	6172904	6065335	6079458
Oral Pills	5250025	6394793	6866654	6874519
Condoms	17214327	16795452	17308141	18698621

Source: HLFPPT Reports & Website.

From the above table it is clear that the program in India currently relies heavily on female sterilization, which is by far the most dominant method. We have had a sea change in our approach to sterilization whose abuse at an earlier was rightly seen an affront to the dignity of women and their human rights. When balance was restored with the paradigm shift there is evidence of sterilization being accepted by most women. The issue was about its timing it in the individual case either by age or order of birth. There is a danger now of an opposite swing even though the alternative of spacing has yet to command any significant following as mentioned already. However, a balanced view would be to give no overriding emphasis to female sterilization but recognize its huge acceptability among women and at the same time create a menu of choices including vasectomy, and reversible contraceptive methods for women. Spacing methods, however, require complementary attention by providers for placing before users harms and benefits attached to each method without imposing his own values. Some spacing methods may also require greater accountability for outcomes and to ensure quality service would include proper follow up.

The group noted the importance of balance between attention to limiting and spacing methods noting that the latter may demand more commitment of time and effort by providers to make for real life choices.

Expanding the Basket for Choice and Access

Method Mix and Informed Choice

It is recommended by the national commission on population is that with differing needs and preferences among users and a cafeteria of services being available it is important that public information is fully given on the new method and also about the precautions before the launch to minimize controversies based sometimes on misinformation. It is equally necessary to ensure that the choices in contraception remain informed choices in letter and spirit.

Contraceptive needs and preferences of users differ and change over time; therefore, a broad selection of reversible and irreversible methods should be available through public health system, social marketing programs, community based outlets and commercial outlets through which condoms and oral contraceptives could be provided. Permanent methods though should be available with the assurance of qualified medical backup at call at primary health centres, community health centres and hospitals in the public health system, as well as through private practitioners and NGOs participating in partnerships. The addition of injectables, progestin—only pills (for women who are breast feeding), barrier methods, and spermicides should be done after due safety and efficacy testing subject to its initial release in the field being carefully monitored and escorted. The threat of HIV/AIDS and the demand from women's groups for barrier methods make a strong case for including these methods in the basket of contraceptive services. Research shows that each new method added attracts new users, improves contraceptive continuation and, thereby increases contraceptive prevalence. However, in view of past controversies over new contraceptives, which were often spearheaded by women's groups themselves, it will be wise to issue a public information sheet prior to introduction about the tests conducted with results of tests or safety, efficacy, acceptability and costs and subsidies so that misinformation may be less and an informed debate may take place without getting mired into tangential controversies. With a real cafeteria of services, informed choice must form an important element of the programme. Service providers should explain pros and cons of each method and the relative risks involved. This will help users make decisions for selecting contraceptive methods that are most appropriate for them after receiving information on harms and benefits and contraindications of contraceptive methods offered to them. Information should also be provided on what users can expect from service providers with regard to advice, support, supply, treatment, referral, and related services in case of need. It is most essential that there is no attempt to impose the value of the provider while guiding the user.

Need Training or Capacity Building Programme

Again the commission is recommended that special training programs must be organized to inculcate contraceptive safety skills at levels especially for ANM, so that they can help in making informed choices.

The aim of the program is to provide people with the means to achieve their reproductive goals in a healthful manner. Contraceptive safety is an essential requirement to ensure that contraceptive products as well as services are delivered safely. At the very least, those reproductive health problems that are directly related to provision of contraceptive services must be addressed. For example, infections should not be caused or exacerbated by the provision of contraceptive methods. Ensuring service quality and safety is specially important for all surgical procedures. Special care must be taken for inserting intrauterine devices (IUDs), particularly in areas where reproductive tract infections (RTIs) and sexually transmitted infections (STIs) are widely prevalent. All health workers including frontline workers such as auxiliary nurse midwives (ANMs) should be trained to provide informed choice of methods, counseling and follow-up care. If the ANM is expected to insert IUDs at the sub-centre (as is the case in several states), then health sub-centres must be provided with equipment to enable her to effectively perform this procedure. Special training programmes must be organized to ensure that she can develop the skills for inserting IUDs safely

Counseling must Need to Make the Programme Success One

After the users have made their choice of the method, counseling should concentrate mainly on the services and caution which they should receive for proper use of the method. Follow-up services are especially important in the initial period for providing advice and managing side effects. Users should have access to service providers if they receive method-related problems, and should have the freedom to switch methods for which supportive counseling should be provided. It is necessary to plan convenient follow-up contacts with users and encourage them to approach providers at any time opportunity for continuing counseling and education and for discussing related reproductive health issues not dealt with earlier. These visits also provide an opportunity to discuss alternative choices if the user is not satisfied with the current method. Developing effective outreach should be a high program priority if counseling and follow-up services are to be provided, especially in remote areas that are difficult to access.

Male Participation

The group will recommend that special efforts should be made to encourage men to take responsibility for family planning in the context of the importance of having their support for the program in a male dominated society.

Benefits of Choice

Family planning enables individuals and couples to determine the number and spacing of their children—a recognized basic human right. Practical benefits are gained at many levels:

- To individuals, improved maternal and infant health; expanded opportunities for women's education, employment and social participation; reduced exposure to health risks; and reduced recourse to abortion;
- To families, reduced competition and dilution of resources; reductions in household poverty; and more possibility for shared decision-making;
- To the society, accelerated demographic transition; and the opportunity to use the "demographic bonus" to speed economic development.

To be Added by After Compilation

In May 2004, the 57th World Health Assembly adopted the World Health Organization's first strategy on reproductive health. The aim is to accelerate progress towards meeting the Millennium Development Goals and the reproductive health goals of the ICPD and its five-year follow-up.

The strategy identifies five priority aspects of reproductive and sexual health:

- Improving antenatal, delivery, postpartum and newborn care;
- Providing high-quality services for family planning, including infertility services;
- Eliminating unsafe abortion;

- Combating STIs, including HIV, reproductive tract infections, cervical cancer and other gynecological morbidities;
- Promoting sexual health.

The Assembly recognized the ICPD Programme of Action, and urged countries to:

- Adopt and implement the new strategy as part of national efforts to achieve the MDGs;
- Make reproductive and sexual health an integral part of planning and budgeting;
- Strengthen health systems' capacities to provide universal access to reproductive and sexual health care, particularly maternal and neonatal health, with the participation of communities and NGOs;
- Ensure that implementation benefits the poor and other marginalized groups including adolescents and men.

Include all aspects of reproductive and sexual health in national monitoring and reporting

REFERENCES

1. www.hlfppt.org
2. www.mohfw.org
3. www.naco.co.in
4. HLFPPT Office Documents.

6

Population Problems in India

Simanchal Maharana
R.L. Panigrahy

The growth of population is a greatest threat to the country's sovereignty. In terms of the size of population, India occupies second position in the world, i.e. next to China. Our population constitutes nearly 15 per cent of the world's population. The present population of India is far more than the combined population of two biggest powers of the world, i.e. U.S.A. and U.S.S.R.

If the size of population is more than what can be absorbed by the national product, it deals to a number of problems. For example, over population results an acute shortages and scarcities which slowing down the process of capital formation affecting balance of trade, lesser number of jobs than required, etc.

Clark argues that a classification of underdeveloped countries shows those with highest rates of population growth have the highest rate of increase of population per head and that historically periods population growth usually precede and provides economic growth.

Easter suggested that population pressure can favourably affect individual motivation and lead to change in production techniques which overcome the consequence of population pressure.

Baser argues that a major stimulus to the green revolution has come from the pressure of population or food supply.

The consequence of population growth on economic development have attracted the attention of economists ever since Adam Smith wrote his Wealth of Nations. He wrote "The annual labour of every nation is the fund which originally supply it with all the necessaries and conveniences of life.

However, the consequences of population growth on development of less developed countries are not the same because the conditions prevailing in these countries are quite different from those the developed economies. These economies are poor, capital scarce and labour abundant population growth adversely affects their economic development in the following ways.

1. Faster population growth makes the choice more scarce between higher consumption now and the investment needed to bring higher consumption in future. Economic development depends upon investment. In less developed countries the sources available for investment are limited. Therefore, rapid growth of population retards investment needed for higher future consumption
2. Rapid population growth tends to over use the natural resources of a country. This is particularly the case where the majority of people are dependent on the sector for their livelihood, e.g. agriculture in India, with rapidly growing population, agricultural holdings became smaller and unremunerative to cultivate.
3. With rapidly growing population it became difficult to manage the adjustments, which accompany economic and social change, urbanisation in less developed countries creates such problems as housing, power, water, transport, etc. Besides growing population threats permanent environmental damage through urbanisation in some rural areas.

However, the rising trend of population in our country is really a matter of great anxiety. It is variable population explosion which is much more dreadful than the atomic explosion. In fact, with a huge population, the country face difficulty in making any crucial dent on its other economic problems like poverty, inequality, and unemployment.

Table 6.1: Growth of population in India (1901-1991)

Census	Population in Million	Increase or Decrease (in Million)	Percentage increase or decrease	Density per sq.km.
1	2	3	4	5
1901	136	0.0	0.0	77
1911	252	+1.6	+5.7	82
1921	251	-1	-0.3	81
1931	279	+28	+11.0	90
1941	319	+40	+14.2	103
1951	361	+42	+13.3	117
1961	439	+78	+21.5	142
1971	548	+109	+24.8	177
1981	685	+137	+25.0	216
1991	834	+62	+23.50	267

Source: Census of India Report.

Table 6.2: Rural-urban population in India (1901-1991)

Year	Rural areas		Urban areas	
	Per cent of people B.P.L.	Number of person (crores)	Per cent of people B.P.L.	Number of person (crores)
1973-74	56.44	26.13	49.01	6.00
1977-78	53.07	26.43	45.24	6.47
1983-84	45.65	25.20	40.79	7.09
1987-88	40.09	23.19	38.20	7.52
1993-94	37.27	24.40	32.36	7.63

Source: Census of India Report

N.B.: B.P.L. Implies Below Poverty Line.

Table 6.3: India's rural-urban population growth (1951-91)

Population Related Figures	*1951*	*1961*	*1971*	*1981*	*1991*
Total population in (million)	361.1	439.2	548.2	685.2	846.3
Rural population (million)	298.7	360.3	439.1	525.7	628.7
Urban population (million)	64.4	78.9	109.1	159.5	217.6
Share of rural population to total (per cent)	82.7	82.0	80.1	76.7	74.3
Share of urban population to total (per cent)	17.3	18.0	19.0	23.3	25.7
Decadal total population growth (per cent)	13.3	21.6	24.8	25.0	23.5
Decadal rural population growth (per cent)	NA	20.6	21.9	19.8	19.6
Decadal urban population growth (per cent)	20.4	26.4	37.9	46.0	36.0
Rural density of population (per sq.km.)	NA	NA	NA	165	200
Urban density of population (per sq.km.)	NA	NA	NA	3000	4092

Disparity in Birth, Death and Mortality Rates

The fact that birth rate in India has always remained substantially higher than urban birth rate by more or less a constant degree or difference clearly shows a poor level of achievement of the population control target in rural areas. This is the main reason for low level of living and poor quality of life of the rural population. Thus, while rural birth rate per thousand of population per annum fell from 39.9 in 1971 to 30.7 in 1992 as against rural death rate declining from 16.4 to 10.8 in the same period, the urban birth rate registered a fall from 30.1 in 1971 to 23.1 in 1992 as against the urban death rate following from 9.7 to 7.0 in the same period. Again, the faster rate of decline in the rural-urban death rate differential from 6.7 per thousand to 3.8 per thousand during 1971-92 than the rate of decline in rural-urban birth rate differential from 8.8 to 7.6 in the same period amply signifies that the average size of rural family through there has been same improvement in child health care in the rural areas (Refer Table—6.4).

Health Facilities

The rural urban difference with respect to health facilities also presents an unhappy picture. It is well known that about 75 per cent of India's population live in rural areas and 25 per cent in urban areas. However, the number of hospitals and dispensaries in rural areas surprisingly works out to just 47 per cent and 74 per cent respectively of the numbers available in urban areas. The number of hospitals and dispensaries per lakh of population accounts for 2.4 in rural areas as against 10.8 in urban areas while that of hospital and dispensary beds together works out to 22 in rural areas and 241 in urban areas.

Table 6.4: Birth rate, death rate and mortality rate (1951-92)

Items & Units of measurement per 1,000 population	*1951*	*1971*	*1981*	*1991*	*1992*
Rural birth rate	NA	38.9	35.6	30.9	30.7
Urban birth rate	NA	30.1	27.0	24.3	23.1
Total birth rate	39.9	36.9	33.9	29.5	29.2
Rural death rate	NA	16.4	13.7	10.6	10.8
Urban death rate	NA	9.7	7.8	7.1	7.0
Total death rate	27.4	14.9	12.5	9.8	10.0
Rural infant mortality rate	NA	138	119	87	85
Rural infant mortality rate	NA	82	62	53	53
Total infant mortality rate	146	129	110	80	79

Source: Economic Survey 1996-97 Govt of India.

Note: @- Per thousand live births.

N.A. Not available.

However, the high infant mortality rate in rural areas not only indicates that the level of medical and health care of people in general and of expectant mothers in particular is low but also signifies that the nutritional content in diet pattern of the rural people is very poor.

Table 6.5: Health facility in India

Description of items	*Hospitals*	*Dispensaries*	*Hospital beds*	*Dispensary beds*
Total number in Rural areas	3.568	11.670	1,26,474	13,133
Total number in Urban area	7.606	15.761	5,15,729	8,799
Per lakh population				
Population in rural areas	0.57	1.86	20.17	2.09
In urban areas	3.50	7.26	237.44	4.05

Source: Basic statistics relating to Indian economy, CMIE, Bombai, Aug' 1994.

Drift Towards Poverty

Table—6.6 show that the population growth rate in urban areas is generally one and a half times that of overally population growth during the last three decades and this trend is to continue up to the year 2000. Section I of Table—6.7 confirms this trend that the percentage of urban population has been increasing in almost all major regions of the world, but in addition it also tells us the ratier starting fact that the drift from rural population to urban has been at the most rapid pace during the last three decades in Africa. Section II of the same table depicts that the increase in urbanisation is the greatest in same of those countries where the drift towards poverty and distress has been the worst. The phenomenon of urbanisation increasing not as a result of improvement of life but as a result of poverty. Famine, distress and violence is most clearly seen in these countries. In Mozambique, for instance, urban population has increased from just 4.6 per cent to 34.3 per cent within three decades. Section III of the same table shows how the percentage of urban population has changed in South Asia and China. This has increased no doubt, but still these countries remain predominantly rural countries.

Table 6.6: Population growth rate

	Total population (annual growth rate)	*Urban population (annual growth rate)*
	Section I (1960-93 project)	
Developing countries	2.2	3.8
Industrial countries	0.8	1.4
World	1.9	2.7
India	2.2	3.4
	Section II (1933-2000 project)	
Development countries	1.8	3.5
Industrial countries	0.4	0.7
World	1.5	2.5
India	1.8	3.0

Source: Human Development Report, 1996.

Cause of Rapid Growth of Population

The relationship of the level of economic development in the growth of population in the Indian contest is examined as follows:

1. *Early and universal marriage:* The practice of marriage is both a religious and social ceremony, which is the potent reason of the rapid increase of population of India. About 80 per cent girls are married during the most fertile period of 15 to 20 years of age. According to the study made by Prof. N.C.D. Das, women marring between 20 and 24 have the same fertility as those marring before the age of 20.
2. *Joint Family System:* It is still prevalent in the large part of the country which support to population growth; despite the fact it has been started disintegration in big cities, even then this system is the common feature.
3. *Widespread Property:* Another fact responsible for rapid growth of population is the wide spread poverty. In India per capita income is very low as compared to other advanced countries nearly 40 per cent of the population

is below the poverty line. Even those who are not below the poverty line are denied nutritious food and other amenities of life. An eminent sociologist Mahmood Mantani observed that while rich farmers invest in machines, the poor at the same time have to invest on their children. So family planning is not accepted among the young couples especially among the low in-come groups.

4. *Religious and social superstitions:* According to Hindu ideology, it is considered one's dharma to have children. In any case they must have a son because certain religious duties will be performed only by him and none else. Similarly they should also have a daughter, as the giving of daughter in marriage is an act of high religious spirit. So these emotional attitudes are based on wrong religious and social norms. In Muslim tradition the birth of a child is considered as a gift of God. So they do not stop their reproductive system.

5. *Lack of Education:* Due to lack of education population are highly increases. As a mass of population are uneducated they can not take keen initiative in scientific education. As a result they will remain backward follower this old religious tradition. In India only 36.17 per cent population is illiterate according to census of India 1991.

6. *Predominance of Agriculture:* It is also another problem of rise in population. In India more than 70 per cent of people depend in agriculture, because it is a agriculture country. There is no second opinion to say that agricultural economies are generally backward, over populated and faced with the problem of disguised un employment.

7. *Decline in Mortality Rate:* Lack of Education: As average number of people are illiterate and backward, their standard of living is very low as compared to others who are well educated and advanced. In backward areas most of the people are not educated. They earn something, they are married, they consider it as a mean of entertainment and they have no other way to recreation. So, in this way the population increases highly.

8. *Decline in Mortality Rate:* The gap between the birth and death rate has considerably resulted in population explosion in the country. The death rate has declined due to control over many dreadful diseases viz. plague malaria small pox, typhoid and tuberculoses. The growing of awareness of facilities for sanitation and cleanliness has helped to reduce the incidence of mortality.

9. *Control of Famines, Floods, and other natural calamities:* During the early years of 19th centuries India witnessed countless famines and floods in the country. The Govt's capacity to cope with the conditions was highly recommended as it faced without import of food stuffs through the production of foodgrains.

10. *Slow Process of Urbanisation:* The slow process of urbanisation is another cause of the rapid growth of population. In India the pace of industrialisation is very slow which further slows down the process of urbanisation in the country. According to 1987 census urban population has been recorded 23.78 per cent against 17.6 per cent in 1951.

11. *Miscellaneous Reasons:* Besides above arguments, there are other reasons responsible for rapid growth of population as bigamy, the climate for male child. Moreover, net reproductive rate is also as high 1.5 per cent while in other countries.

    In fact, it is clear that India is presently, passing through a period of population explosion due to her continuing high birth rates and sharp decline in the mortality rate.

12. *Food Supply:* The net availability of food grains (cereals) increased from 63 million tonnes in 1956 to more than 170 million tonnes in 1989-90. During the same period population increases from 397 millions to about more than 800 million. If the present trend in increase in population continues the population of the country would reach about 1000 million by the end of the century.

13. *Growth of National Income:* The national income rose by more than 300 per cent during 1950-51 to 1990-91,but on account of increase in population the per capita income rose by 85 per cent only.

14. *Problem of Unemployment:* The net addition to the labour force during the period 1992-97 is estimated to be 35 million and another 36 million will be expected to an addition during 1997-2002. Thus, additional employment opportunities of the order of 58 million will have to be created during 1992-1997 if the goal of near full employment is to be reached in 1997.

    As the growth of population is very fast, the number of labour force entered in population as labour force seek employment. In developing countries, the job is very less than the job seekers. So, not only unemployment but also the underemployment, disguised unemployment and the engagements without remuneration (which can not be called as employment as the definition of employment) are found in India. So, what a miserable condition of the productive group of Indian population are lying neglected. It is the wastage of Indians human resources. Due to unemployment the social problems also occur. The unemployment youth many times commits notorious works like mischief in streets, public places, pick-pocketing, comment to the young girls, rape, theft, murder, love harassment effects, smuggling, prostitution, drink etc. The unemployment multiplies lowering the growth rate of the economy of the country. Due to unemployment the per capita income of the country declines.

15. *Capital Formation:* According to Dale & Hoove, "the rapid growth of population tend to diminish the amount of capital available for investment and production diminishes". According to Prof. Leibenstein, "in densely populated economies, population growth is an obstacles to development because it dilutes the amount of capital with the representative worker operate." In India 40 to 50 per cent of its population are in unproductive group

and unemployment arises from the productive age group of 15 to 50 years. So, Prof. Meier has noticed that, "the high dependency requires the economy to divert considerable part of the resources that might otherwise go into capital formation to the maintenance of high percentage of dependents who may never become producers". Thus, the rapid growth of population leads to diversion of capital investment from direct activities to social overhead capital.

16. *Population and social infrastructure:* Rapidly growing population require large investment in social infrastructure and diverts resources from directive product assists. Due to scarcity of resources, it is not possible to provide education, health, medical, transport and housing facilities to the entire population. There is over crowding everywhere. As a result, the quality of these services goes down. Large number of mitigate against an improvement in the quality of the population as productive agent. The rapid increases in school-age population and an extending number of labour forces entrants put ever grater pressure on educational and training facilities and retard improvement in the quality of education.

17. *Ecological Degradation:* Rapid growth of population in India, as in many other countries is somewhat upset, the ecological balance. There is a gradual shrinking or covered by forces as also upon land denudation of forest means serious soil erosion and floods with their diverts consequence of food production. Rapid population growth leads to environmental damages scarcely of land due to rapid increasing population pushes large number of ecological sensitive areas such as hill sides and tropical forests.

18. *Population and World Economy:* Rapid population growth effects and less developed countries in relation to the world economy in a number of ways. Rapid population growth trends to increase income disparities between less developed countries and developed countries because

per capita income decline with population growth to the rapid population growth increases international migration.

Demographic Profile of India

Population is the source of the most important factor of production, labour, labour acts upon and makes use of other factor of production. Scarcity of labour may compel a country to scale down its rate of economic growth. Indeed it has happened so with a number of countries, especially France, Australia, etc. But if the population grows at an uncontrolled rate, it may not prove good for the country. It may not only restrict the process of economic growth but may also nullify all the process that a country might have made in the economic sphere.

Some Basic Facts—Relating to India's Population

1. *Size and Growth Rate of Population in India:* A study of the growth of population of India falls three distinct phases—the first phase of 30 years from 1891 to 1921, the second phase from 1921 to 1951, another period of 30 years and third phase of 30 years from 1951-1981. During 1891 to 1921 the population of India grew from 236 million in 1891 to 251 million in 1921 i.e. just by 15 million. During the second phase of 30 years 1921 to 1951 the population of India grew from 251 million in 1921 to 361 million in 1951. i.e. by 110 million. The compound growth rate of population was 1.22 per cent per annum which can be considered as moderate.

The main reason for the increase in population growth rate was a decline in death rate from about 49 per thousand to 27 per thousand, but compared with this, there was a very small decrease in birth rate.

During the third phase of 30 years (1951-1981) the population of India grew from 361 million in 1951 to 683 million in 1981. This gives a compound rate of annual growth to be 2.14 per cent.

Table 6.7: Crude birth and death rate

(Per 100 populations)

Census Year	Growth Rate	Birth Rate	Death Rate
. 1991-1911	NA	49.2	42.6
1911-1921	NA	48.1	47.2
1921-1931	NA	46.4	36.2
1931-1941	NA	45.2	31.2
1941-1951	NA	41.7	27.4
1951-1961	NA	37.2	19.0
1961-1971	6.6	41.2	19.0
1971-1981	0.9	37.2	15.0
1981-1985	10.1	32.2	11.7
1985-1987	14.0	32.9	11.8
1987-1988	12.5	32.6	11.1
1988-1989	18.9	32.2	10.9
1989-1990	22.2	31.6	11.0
1990-1991	22.5	30.5	10.2
1991-1992	21.0	29.9	9.6

Source: Pocket Book of Population Statistics, Census of India 1981, 1992.

The most encouraging feature of the demographic scene in India is that the birth rate has begin to fall. It is estimated to have come down to 31.5 at the beginning of the 8th plan in April 1990. The birth rate is targeted to come down to 23.1 in 1999-2000. Along with the birth rate, the death rate is targeted to fall to 8.9 in 1999-2000, giving a natural growth rate of population of 14.2 per thousand in 1999-2000.

Statewise analysis of data pertaining to birth and death rates reveals that Kerala, Tamil Nadu, A.P., W.B., Himanchal Pradesh, Karnataka, Maharasthra, Punjab, Gujarat and Assam have achieved a birth rate below 30 per thousand.

Fertility depends upon (i) age at which females marry, (ii) duration of the period of fertile union and (iii) the rapidity with which they build their families. In India the age at which female marry is very low despite the efforts made by the Govt. in bringing a number of legislation. Because of early marriage, the period of fertile union is large and consequently the rapidity is also high.

High birth rate due to many reasons e.g. (i) universal marriage, (ii) men and women marry at quite an early age, (iii) the majority of population is illiterate, orthodox and superstitions further they are religious minded and for that male child is a must. Average Indian family is quite poor, and as a consequence addition of every child in the family is welcome . It is a helping hand and sources of income to family. So the birth rate in India is high.

2. *Age composition:* While analysing the effect of population growth on labour supply , we should know the distribution of population according to age. The study of age composition is helpful in determining the proportion of the labour force in the total population. The working age of population is considered to be 15 to 60.

Table 6.8: Age structure projection (As on 1st March' 2001)

Age group	*1980*	*1985*	*1990*	*2000 (per cent)*
0-4	14.18	13.19	12.85	10.67
5-14	25.54	24.34	23.15	20.96
15-59	54.07	55.51	57.50	60.79
Above 60	6.21	6.24	6.50	7.58
Total	**100.00**	**100.00**	**100.00**	**100.00**

It would be seen that in India only about 55 per cent of the total population is in the working age group of 15-59 years. The balance of 45 per cent of the total population constitutes the group of dependents.

3. *Sex Composition:* By sex ratio we mean the number females per thousand males. From the point of view of sex ratio, India's position is quite different as compared to other countries. The sex ratio has declined from 934 in 1981 to 929 in 1991.

Table 6.9: Sex composition in India (1901-2001 census)

Year of Census	*Female in 1000 males*
1901	972
1911	968
1921	955
1931	950
1941	945
1951	946
1961	940
1971	932
1981	935
1991	929
2001	972

This table shows that the number of female per one thousand male steadily downward sloping rapidly.

4. *Life Expectency:* The living age in which the inhabitants of a nation are expected at the time of birth is known as expectation of life. The mortality rate of India is stated below.

Year	*Life Expectancy*
1921	19.4
1931	26.9
1941	32.0
1951	33.0
1961	41.0
1971	52.0
1981	54.0
1991	59.0

The above table depicts that life expectancy in India is very low.

5. *Literacy:* As a basic human need, education helps in acquiring a broad base of knowledge, attitudes, values and skills. The quality of population can be judged from life expectancy, the level of literacy and the level of technical training attained by the people of a country.

The Directive Principles of State Policy regarding universalization of elementary education our Constitution has made provision under Article 45 that " The State shall endeavour to provide, within a period of ten free and compulsory education for all children until they complete the age of 14 years." The following chart gives a clear picture as to how for we are from our objectives.

Literacy Rate in India 1951-1991

Year	*Persons (%)*	*Male (%)*	*Female (%)*
1951	18.33	27.16	8.86
1961	28.31	40.40	15.34
1981	43.56	56.37	29.75
1991	52.11	63.86	39.42

The total literacy rate in the country is 52.11 per cent the males, it is 63.86 per cent and the females lag behind with 39.42 per cent, only Kerala has the maximum male and female literacy as per the 1991 census 94.45 per cent in males and 86.93 per cent in females.

6. *Density of Population:* India is one of the high-density countries of the world. Density refers to population per square kilometre. It is the total population divided by total area. Density of population is used for information about land-man ratio. With land are remaining almost stable, and the country's population rising rapidly; the density of population in India has been increasing very fast.

Density of population, 1921-1991

Year	*Density* *No. of persons per square km.*
1921	79
1931	88
1941	100
1951	113
1961	138
1971	177
1981	216
1991	267

The following are the facts, which influence the density of population in the country:

1. Agricultural facilities
2. Industrial Development
3. State of Economic Development
4. Peace and security.

REFERENCES

1. Bhattanagar, P.N.-*Social Studies*, Dhanpat Rai & Co., Delhi.

7

Population and Moral Degradation

Balakrishna Padhi
Premananda Pradhan

India today possess about 2.4 per cent of the total land area of the world. At the beginning of the century India's population was 236 million and according to 1991 census, the population of India is 844 million. According to 2001 census report, the population of India is 102 crores. A study of growth rate of India's population falls into four phases.

1891-1921 : Stagnant population
1921-1951 : Steady growth
1951-1981 : Rapid high growth
1981-2001 : High growth with definite signs of slowing down

The frightening growth rate of population has been shown in the following:

Table 7.1: (1990-2001)

Census year	*Total (in crores)*	*Average annual Growth rate (%)*	*Decadal Growth rate (%)*
1	2	3	4
1901	23.84	–	–
1911	25.20	0.56	5.75

(Table Contd...)

1	2	3	4
1921	25.13	(-) 0.03	-0.31
1931	27.89	1.04	11.00
1941	31.86	1.33	14.22
1951	36.10	1.25	13.31
1961	43.92	1.96	21.51
1971	54.82	2.20	24.80
1981	68.33	2.22	24.66
1991	84.63	2.14	23.85
2001	102.70	1.93	21.34

Source: Registrar General of India.

The above table exhibits that the growth rate of population is expanding day by day at an alarming rate. Comparing to 1991 and 2001 census, there is additions of 18.1 crores of population. This frightening growth rate of population has aggravated the problems of poverty, unemployment, sub-human life and inequalities. Besides, there has been neglect of social sectors like primary education, basic health and social security. It has been found that high growth of population has made rural-urban migration. Since the rural sector fails to provide adequate job avenues to the rural surplus labour, hence they migrate to urban areas. Besides, there is high expectation of income and employment is ensured. The Table—7.2 shows rural urban migration in India.

Table 7.2: (1990-2001)

Year	*Population (in crores)*		*Size in total population (%)*	
	Rural	*Urban*	*Rural*	*Urban*
1	*2*	*3*	*4*	*5*
1901	21.3	2.5	89.2	10.8
1911	22.6	2.6	89.2	10.3
1921	22.3	2.8	88.8	11.2
1931	24.5	3.4	88.0	12.0
1941	27.4	4.4	86.1	13.9

(Table Contd...)

1	2	3	4	5
1951	29.8	6.3	82.7	17.3
1961	36.0	7.9	82.0	18.0
1971	43.9	10.9	80.1	19.9
1981	52.4	15.9	76.7	23.3
1991	62.9	21.7	74.3	25.7
2001	74.2	28.5	72.2	27.8

Source: Registrar General of India.

Table 7.3: Population in large cities

Cities	*Population in 1991 (in Million)*	*Population in 1981 (in Million)*
1. Greater Mumbai	12.6	8.2
2. Calcutta	10.9	9.2
3. Delhi	8.4	5.7
4. Madras	5.4	4.3
5. Ahmedabad	3.3	2.5
6. Bangalore	4.1	2.5

Besides, the above mega cities the high concentration of population is also found in Surat, Kochi, Madurai, Bhopal, Visakhapatnam, etc.

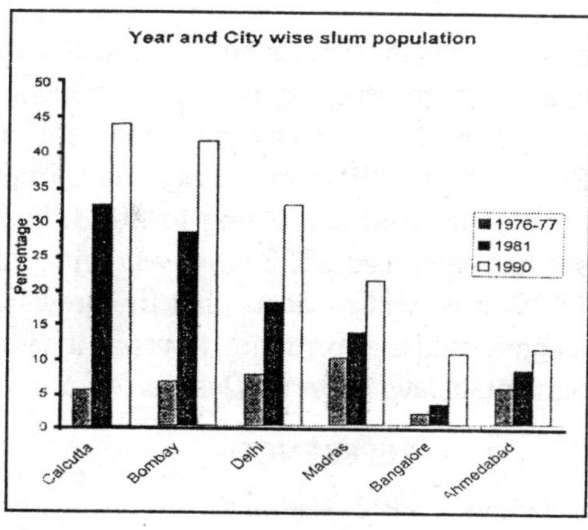

DIAGRAM–1

From the above bar-diagrams it is revealed that the large influx of rural migrants has generated the problem of slum. They took shelter in the road side in the small cottages which are purely unhygienic. The rural migrant population are associated with several antisocial activities like robbery, murder, pick-pocketing, kidnapping, theft, sexual relations, etc. Ultimately this has eroded the moral values. Hence, there is moral degradation. Both the forward linkage and backward linkage of rural urban population has polluted both the rural as well as urban societies. Selfish nature, greedy, prodigality, showiness and modern fashion grasps the rural belts.

Individualism virtues like goodness, truth altruistic attitude, moral and spiritual conduct which were the treasure of Indian culture, have been mercilessly butchered on the altar of so-called development and modernisation. The principle of "live and let live" has disappeared. In its place a "me first" culture has been developed. A transient culture self centred of hedonism has replaced the perennial culture of humanism.

It is cultural, spiritual and moral chord which provides the support system, the strength and vitality to human development. Once this chord is severed and the vitality is lost, the social and economic system will be in jeopardy.

In the aforesaid context it is suggested that until and unless moral development is possible, the tempo of economic growth plus welfare would be zero.

It has been noticed in the various news papers that the trend of corruption is alarmingly growing day by day. Corruption including pick-pocketing, murder, theft, kidnapping is rampant prevalence. According to 2004 report, at Berhampur city, the corruption trend has increased to 25 per cent comparing to 2003. In 2003, the number of cases has been filed 1552 whereas during 2004 it has increased to 1898. It is vividly evident that the growing trend of population has aggravated the corruption level and it has compelled to the Govt. to maintain law, order and justice.

REFERENCES

1. Datta, R. & Sundaram, K.P.M.—*Indian Economy*.

2. *Journal of Orissa Economic Association*, 2000 Issue.

3. Jhingan, M.L.; Bhatt, B.K. & Desai, J.N.-*Demography*, Vrinda Publications (P) Ltd., ND.

4. *The Sambad*, Oriya Daily, Dated 6th Jan' 2004.

8

Indian Human Rights Commission
A Juncture

Dr. Dasarathi Bhuyan

In 1993 India serendipitously, discovered the urgency for the establishment of a Human Rights Commission. It was a pity that the prime motivation for this Human Rights Commission was formed by foreign pressure, not fresh concern for halting the horror of human rights violation. The official paper, with unblushing candour, discloses why now this commission. There has been a growing awareness in the country and abroad about issues relating to human rights. National and International organisations in this field have been highlighting alleged violations of human rights by various government functionaries. There is a growing feeling that the government is not serious about such violations and excesses and bringing the guilty persons to book.

Prime Minister P. V. Narasimha Rao, at the conference of the Chief Ministers on the September 1992 sensitively spoke of commitment to upholding human rights, "we must send a clear message that we do not tolerate violation of human rights". Painfully aware of the shortcomings of the government vis-à-vis protection of human rights, he conceded that "there is need to identify the weakness, the gaps between pronouncement and action and between legislation and its implementation". The truth was that within and without the country the governments credibility about human rights commitment was at a low ebb, low ever since the emergency, lower during the Rajiv regime and lowest during these bad days of operation liquidation using guileful denominations.

It was reported that forest secretary's office had perhaps not been to happy with Dr. L.M.Singvi for his enthusiastic expression of the need for an Indian Human Rights Commission, a commitment that the Congerss party had already made in its last election manifesto.

Dr. Singvi, the distinguished High Commissioner in Britain has been an outstanding humanist and human rights activist at the national and international levels and his stature and convictions gave him non option but to mention the imperative need for a commission in defence of human rights. In this regard he was higher than his office. He had been aware of the demonstrations in Europian capitals, perhaps influenced by Amnesty International reports on India's record of human rights violation. Abid Hussain, representing India in America—a country with bankrupt credentials to sermonize human rights must have had the painful experience of criticism levelled against India in Washington on the human rights front. On June 26, 1992 the Burton Bill had been passed by the House of Representative which called for a cut from the development assistance account meant for India and some other third world countries. This cut was an index of American unease at India's increasing human rights infractions. Certainly, the USA could easily create international moral opinion against mendicant India and the donor countries would on this score have turned a deaf ear to India's need for foreign aid.

Inside the country, there had been considerable vocal assusations by social action groups, civil liberties organisations and sensitive souls scattered all over the country, about the atrocities by the police and the army and allied agencies on men, women and children, often innocent, using various alibis, apart from escalating frequency of routine torture inside custodial institutions. Foreign criticism, for an aid-sustained nation like India, hurts its soft underside, especially when the Prime Minister and the Finance Minister run the economy on doles and debts with humiliating conditionalities.

In this black background, the Prime Minister's rush response to adverse comments from abroad to meet it with make believe outfit demands a sceptical scrutiny. When a question arises to set up

Human Rights Commission he argued, why ? Not necessarily to wipe out the savage violations by state-clad miscreants, feudal felons, communal black guards maniacs, mafia and other rural-urban lawless elements, but to colour was crimes by trigger happy or torturesome police or rapist savages in uniform and counter them by the specious plea that terrorist groups are the real great offenders.

Shri J.N.Dixit, Indian Foreigh Secretary has coincidentally told US Senators and Congressmen in Washington about the formation of an Indian Human Rights Commission. Such a body, Dixit informed would ally apprehensions about India's human rights violations to the international community.

There is a pathological insincerity, an unethical allergy and anxiety to cover up, writ large in the defensive manoeuvre of a human rights commission ploy. The contrition of a culprit state and the determination to conscientise delinquent state violators is absent and an amnesia about the Delhi program of 1984, the Jharkhand, Chatisgarh, Bihar killing; Bodo brutalities indiscriminate human liquidations in Punjab and Kashmir and Assam under variously labelled 'operations', the barbarities and the homicidal, sexuberant havoc of the army and allied forces in the north east, not to speak of the terrorism of TADA, the 'disappearances' and 'police encounters' and shoot at sight orders shockingly exercised without the law and bereft of any sense of compassion rouses the range of anyone with heart. Tortures by the police, prison privations and other custodial crimes galore are too poignant for tears. When the sage of human rights in India is chronicled objectively by political scientists, the insensitive escalation of state turpitude and culpable torture, rape and massacre inflicted by the police and the army, winked at by the ministry, the fewer pages that better for the political-administrative echelons in power. The police in action and even collaboration in crimes against women and dalits and dissenters is an untold story of enormity. That other countries have worse records or that terrorism can not be obliterated without armed brutality by the state is too shocking to be urged in civilized fore.

Amnesty International has been consistently critical of India's performance as of others. For instance, Assian Report wrote in London:

"The killings of civilians can never be accepted. The deliberate massacre of a particular community by another is as horrendous as the state killing innocent people."

Human Rights are crucial significance and are essential to human welfare and prosperity. They are designed to enhance the status of the individual in society in which he lives and to provide him with safeguards which are considered necessary for his protection against the arbitrary authority of the state.

Being advised by the United Nations and international forums India has established National Human Rights Commission with the mandate to enquire into allegations of human rights violations and take necessary measures to prevent these crimes. The commission is trying to build human rights culture in the country since its establishment in 1993.

India's Human Rights can be viewed as the third world perspective of human rights, because it mainly revolves around the concept of development. It is evident from the trend followed by these countries at the various international and national forums. These countries have raised issues relating to civil and political rights, but there is tilt towards social, economic and cultural rights is too obvious. The third world finds more attraction in the collective expression of human rights as opposed to the view of the developed world, which is over concerned with individual and political rights for the promotion of its own selfish interest.

India's approach to human rights is a balanced one which views the rights of the individual in a comprehensive framework of social, economic and political development.

9

Population and Impact of Women Health

(A Study of Ganjam District)

Dr. P.K. Patnaik

According to the 2001 census India's population is 102.10 crores and 84.40 crores and 68.3 crores in 1991 census respectively. The population India of substantially rise 14.4 crores within two decades (1981-2001 census). We will cross the mark of a thousand million by the turn of twentieth century of current rate of growth and would be double of that in the next 35 years. We are increasing at a rate of 16 million a year 479871 per day, 48 births are taking place in every minutes, within 2.4 per cent of the world area we are supporting 16 per cent of the world population. The implication are mind boggling.

Women's health status is basic to their advance in all fields of endeavour. Though health of women has been identified for priority attention and efforts made for maternal and child survives since the planned development in India much remains to be done to improve health care for women both in qualitative and quantitative terms. The sex-ratio which illumines the survival scene for women versus men was 972 females per 1000 males in 2001 census. Not only is this ratio unfavourable but its steady decline is a course for great concern women face high risk of malnutrition, retardation in growth and development disease, disability and even death at three critical stages in their lives viz. infancy, early childhood and reproductive phase.

During the last 59 years for independence, the rural primary public health infrastructure has recorded an impressive increase. The network consists of 1,45,000 sub-centres, 22,700 primary health centre and 3222 community health centres. Catering to a population of 5,000, 3,000 and 11,00,000 respectively land 3000, 20,000 and 80,000 population in tribal and deserve areas. In fact, the country has achieved impressive demographic transition through the decline of Crude Birth Rate (CBR), Crude Death Rate (CDR), Total Fertility Rate (TFR) and Infant Mortality Rate (IMR). However, the existence of sharp disparities in key public health indicators and inequalities even among the better performing states pose challenges to the development of India's health sector.

The Govt. of India has enacted a National Rural Health Mission on 12th April, 2005. The mission covers the entire country with special focus on 18 states where the challenge of strengthening weak public health system and improving key health indicators is the highest. These studies include Uttar Pradesh, Madhya Pradesh, Bihar, Rajasthan, Orissa, Uttaranchal, Jharkhand, Chatisgarh, Assam, Arunchal Pradesh, Mizoram, Nagaland, Sikkim, Tripura, Jammu & Kashmir and Himachal Pradesh. The mission aims at provision of integrated comprehensive and effective primary health care to the poor and vulnerable, and marginalised sections of the society, especially women and children by improving access, availability, quality and accountability of public health services. The duration of the mission is 7 years from 2005-2012.

At the National level, the mission steering group chaired by Union Minister shall lay down the guiding principles and policies for the mission. The Department of Health and Family Welfare (H & FW), Youth Affairs (YA), Women and Child Development (W & CD), Panchayati Raj, Rural Development (RD), Drinking Water Supply, North East Region and 10 nominated public health professional are represented in the mission steering group. An empowered programme committee chaired by Secretary (H & W) shall implement the mission.

At the state level, the Chief Minister shall lead the State Health Mission which shall be co-chaired by the Health Minister. The existing societies under vertical programmes of H & FW shall be integrated into the society. The state programme management unit equipped with skilled professional manpower shall provide the secretarial support to the health mission.

Early state shall prepare an integrated State Action Plan for RCH-II, National Disease Surveillance Programmes and related sectors of nutrition, sanitation and hygiene release of funds to state shall be based on achievement of core performance indicators reflected by the State Government in its Action Plan. At all the levels, the focus of the mission shall be to address vulnerable population groups and under served areas.

Health Policy

In accordance with the health policy of 2005 provision has been made for providing health care for all by the turn of this century. Through manufacturing of new medicines have helped us to wipe out infectious diseases like small pox, polio and to some extent malaria. Though the rate of mortality has been reduced to a considerable extent and average lifespan has gave up to 60 years in the country. Yet it is deplorable that malnutrition among the women and children in poorer states of society has caused deep concern. Therefore, maternal and child health care has been accorded specially providing in the primary health services. Government has launched varieties of programme like universal immunisation programme, diarrhoea diseases control programme. Prevention of nutritional scarcity, etc. for the children which are integral part of maternal and child health services.

Demographic Profile of Orissa

The total population of Orissa as on March 2001 was 36,706,920 according to the provisional census 2001 with a decadal growth rate of 15.94 per cent which is lower than the decadal growth rate of India (21.34%). This constitute 3.57 per cent of the total population of India as per 2001 census 3.5 per cent of population of Orissa resides in an area of 155,707 sq. kms. As per 2001 census, the sex ratio female per thousand male was 972 and 971 in 1991 census. There are also variations in sex ratio in different districts of Orissa. Gajapati district has recorded the highest sex ratio of 1031 during 2001. The lowest sex ratio of 901 has been observed in the district of Khurda.

Health Services in Orissa

The state of Orissa through a network of three medical colleges, 30 district headquarter hospitals, 146 sub-divisional hospitals, 158 community health centres, 1166 primary health centres, 197 mobile health units, 522 ayurvedic hospitals and dispensaries, 480 homeopathic hospitals and dispensaries. The total number of beds for patients available is only 14,036 as on 1.6.2003.

Demographic Profile of Ganjam District

Ganjam district is one of the second highest density populated district next to Khurda district of Orissa. In addition to the total population is highest in the district among 30 districts of Orissa. The Ganjam district has a total population of 31,61,000 lakhs according to 2001 census which constitutes 8.59 per cent of the total population of the state. The decadal growth rate of districts population indicates 19.88 per cent as on 2001 census. The share of male population in the total was 15,2,000 lakhs and the female population in the total was 15,79,000 lakhs as on 2001 census in the Ganjam district. According to 2001 census, the sex ratio shows that these were 998 for 1000 males, the earlier decade (1981 and 1991 census), the sex ratio was 1012 and 1006 females for 1000 males respectively in the district. The district has third position in sex ratio in the state in 1991 census.

Health Services in Ganjam District

The health services in the Ganjam district through network of the one medical college, one district headquarter hospitals, 11 sub-divisional and other hospitals, 10 community health centres, 83 primary health centres, 15 mobile health units, 41 ayurvedic hospitals and dispensaries, 41 homeopathic hospitals and dispensaries with 1541 available beds for patients in these medical units of Ganjam district as on 1.6.2003. There is no tremendous increase in beds afterwards.

The most crucial problem facing the nation today is the population explosion which is underminimise other efforts towards socio-economic development. Under this circumstances the importance of launching the family programme in a mass scale needs no emphasis. The Orissa Government have implemented family welfare programme vigorously to curb the population explosion.

The National Population Policy (NPP), 2000 has been announced during Ninth Plan (1997-2002). The key objective of the NPP, 2000 is to bring down total fertility rates to replacement levels by 2010. The policy aims at reducing infant mortality rate to below thirty per cent births, reducing maternal mortality rate to below 100 per 1,00,000 births achieving universal immunisation of children against all vaccine preventable diseases. The Reproductive Child Health (RCH) programme has continued during Ninth Plan 1997-2002. Several new schemes for improving quality and coverage of services are under implementation.

Family Planning, the Concept

Family planning implies to have children by choice not by chance. It is an instrument of social change. 'Creating better part healthier children and happier home' is the main theme of family planning under the programme, married couple are generally persuaded to limit the size of their family.

Features

1. Eligible couples are motivated to undergo sterilisation operations and to adopt special methods using loop, oral pills, condoms and contraceptives and under advanced methods.
2. The main component of family welfare programme are population control or family planning and immunisation.
3. Financial incentives are given in order to motivate more and more people came under this programme.
4. The entire outlay under the family welfare programme continue to increase since the beginning of the programme for the year 1993-94 an outlay, of Rs. 1270 crores has been approved for the country. The seventh plan

Table 9.1: Family Welfare Programme achievement in the Ganjam District in 1989-90 to 2000-01

Sl. No.	Items	1991-92	1992-93	1993-94	1994-95	1995-96	1996-97	1997-98	1998-1999	1999-2000	2000-01
1.	Sterilisation	13515	12581	11930	13803	13823	13457	10866	9620	8419	7697
2.	I.U.D.	14529	13787	15689	17181	17079	15171	19608	18681	15867	14761
3.	CC users	26041	24577	33121	44416	36177	30690	11037	19762	16222	14424
4.	Oral Pill user	4905	4256	6396	8480	8660	8386	9060	8033	7604	8268
5.	Tetanus Toxide				76696	80272	79402	78853	77774	70791	70481
6.	D.P.T.				74947	74516	77574	79379	77614	37062	75447
7.	Polio				75146	74493	77584	79379	76390	69993	75447
8.	B.C.G.				84338	76787	82700	85206	80188	76152	76514
9.	Measles				71069	60993	73832	68893	66210	53551	61009

Source: Director, Health & Family Welfare, Orissa.

(1985-90) provided an outlay of Rs. 3256 crore for the family welfare programme (FWP). The outlay of the National Rural Health Mission for 2005-06 is Rs. 6731 crore in family welfare programme in India.

The Table—9.1 reveals the phenomenal achievements under family welfare programmes during the year 1991-92 to 2000-2001 (a decade). The item No. 1, sterilisation is constant from 1991-92 to 1996-97 with a slight fluctuation in number. But, the number is decreasing from 1998-99 to 2000-01 (compared 1991-92 to 1996-97. Similarly item No. 2, IUD performance is increasing rate from 1991-92 to 1998-99 with a little number fluctuations. But, after 1990-91 to 2000-01 it is decreased. The performance is highest during the year 1997-98, i.e. 19,608 under the above item. Next, comes to item No. 3, CC users—the number is increasing, but a fluctual rate from 1991-92 to 1996-97. After 1997-98 to 2000-01 it is decreased in diminishing rate. The performance is highest, i.e. 44,416 during the year 1994-95 within a decade. The item No. 4, oral pill users are continuously decreased from 1991-92 to 1992-93. But, it is gradually increased from 1993-94 to 2000-01. The service of tetanus toxide (TT) for pregnant women is increased from 1994-95 to 1998-99. But it is decreased from 1999-2000 to 2000-01 with high rate. The DPT service under family welfare programme is increased from 1994-95 to 2000-01. But this trend is downward during the year 1999-2000. The number is 37,062. The performance of polio service in the district is increased trend from 1994-95 to 2000-01. The health service BCG is highest performance from 1994-95 to 1998-99. But it is decreasing trend during the year 1999-2000 to 2000-01 with a little change in number. Lastly the performance of measles item is increased trend from 1994-95 to 1998-99. But after 1999-2000 to 2000-01 it is slightly different compared to 1994-95 to 1998-99 in the Ganjam district though the data reveals within a decade tremendous success in realising the target but in view of the gravity of problem the success is far from satisfactory. But, it should be checked and balanced with a vigilant way, while service is available in the district.

Suggestions

The following are the suggestions for family welfare programme.

(i) In India the family planning programme has been developed with the main objective controlling population growth, experience has shown that the family planning programme can not succeed unless it is broad based.

(ii) The main determinant of health policy should be literacy, age at marriage, employment opportunities for women, improvement of their situation in the society, reduction of mortality, improving health care, nutrition of pre-school child and producing a comprehensive packages at maternal health care service, political commitment, inter-sectoral interaction and a popular movement.

(iii) Participation of NGO and voluntary organisation should constitute the main strategy to popularise the family planning, educational awareness programmes are to be launched on rural areas. This should be popularised through radio, TV, rally, seminar, workshop, camps, street theatre, drama, folk dance, exhibitions in festivals on family planning issues in rural area especially for the women group. Direct participation of voluntary organisation (VO) can play a vital role in this regard.

(iv) Efforts should be made to motivate the girls to go to schools, acquire skill, marry late and have one or two children.

(v) Effective steps should be taken for employment generation and poverty alleviation in rural areas through self help groups (SHG) in women groups.

(vi) The efforts should be taken for removal of their blind believes, social dogmas and superstitions by the voluntary organisation (VO) and govt. level organisations especially in rural area through different cultural programme and traditional cults.

REFERENCES

1. *Yojana*, Vol. 49, July' 2005, pp. 2-5.
2. *Social Welfare*, Vol. 43, No. 4, July' 1996, p. 3.
3. *Social Welfare*, Vol. XL, No. 7, Oct' p. 23.
4. *Population Studies*—2004, pp. 146-149, 211-212, Elegant Publications, Bhubaneswar.
5. Family Welfare Sectarian, Chief District Medical Office, Ganjam Berhampur.
6. *District Statistical Hand Book*, Ganjam, 1997, 1998, 2001, Dept. of Statistics & Economics, Govt. of Orissa.
7. *District at a Glance*, Orissa 2005, Dept. of Statistics & Economics, Govt. of Orissa.

10

Problems of Agricultural Labour

(A Study of Ganjam District)

Santosh Kumar Pradhan

Introduction

In General, the world labour connotes the physical or mental works that will be dame body in under to get remunerations for his/her social existence. In each and every sphere of production and function, labour has been considered as the ingredient lacuna out of the factor of production. Colin Clerk, one of leading developmental economists stated that, "It is not gold but man makes the nation strong." Despite of its supreme importance the problems of labourers has engulfed the entire developed economic plan. The problems like differential wage structure, low level of literacy, unhygienic economic condition, incidence of poverty has germinated numerous socio-economic problems.

Generally, labourer are engaged in various diversification jobs like mining, construction, forestry, shipping, plantation, fisheries and so on. However, for research analysis the problems of agricultural labourer has been purposively selected.

Labour in Difference Sector

The contribution of labour in the process of production is found to be paramount role. This factor is pervasiveness in different sector of economy such as agriculture (main), industry (secondary), and allied service. As comparing to the allied and industrial sectors labour is highly concentrated in agricultural sector. This is due to the fact that the failure of allied and secondary sector coupled with menacing growth of population.

Labours are also actively engaged in un-organised sector. The term un-organised labour has been defined as those workers who have not been able to organize themselves in pursuit of their common interests, due to certain constraints like causal nature of employment, ignorance and illiteracy, small and scattered size of establishment, etc. are mostly happening in agricultural sector. As per the survey carried out by the National Sample Survey Organisation (NSSO) in year 1999-2000, the total employment in both organized and un-organized sector in the country was of the order of 39.7 corer in construction work, 4.1 corer in manufacturing, 3.7 corer in trade and 3.7 core in transport, communication and other services.

Position of Agriculture Labourer

To have a glance it is almost painstacking to find out and over view about the present scenario of agricultural labourers. A plethora of information are available to support the position of agricultural labourers in India.

Being India is purely Agricultural Economy, a large segment of Indian population depends on agriculture. The census report of 1901 to 2001 it is revealed that the growth rate of population is expanding beyond the psychological expectations, it has increased from 23.6 to 102 crores from 1901 to 2001. Accordingly the number of dependency ratio of population in agricultural sector is upward trend. This is clearly narrated from the agricultural statistics as follows:

The Table—10.1 reveal that in comparison with total labour force in the economy to agricultural labour increase in the country over the years. Whereas the percentage of agricultural worker was 2.4.94 in year 1901 reached to 40.25 per cent in the yeaı 1991 similarly the total number of agricultural labourer was 17.26 millions in 1901 which reached with upto and trend to 74.59 millions in the years 1998. Although the economic reasons have been mainly responsible for such increase in the number of agricultural labourers, social structure have also been a contributory factor to some extent.

Table 10.1: Number of Agricultural Labour (1901-2001) - (in millions)

Year	*Total population*	*Total labour force*	*Agricultural workers*		*Agricultural Labourers%*	
			Agricultural Labourers	*Cultivators*	*Total Workers*	*Agricultural Workers*
1901	236.28	110.71	17.26	51.95	15.59	24.94
1911	252.12	121.30	24.06	58.47	19.84	29.51
1921	251.35	117.75	19.65	61.60	16.69	24.18
1931	279.02	120.67	22.11	57.67	18.33	27.72
1951	361.31	139.42	27.50	69.75	19.72	28.28
1961	439.23	188.68	31.50	99.62	16.71	24.04
1971	547.95	180.37	47.48	78.17	26.33	37.39
1981	665.30	244.60	55.50	92.50	22.69	37.50
1991	838.58	285.93	74.59	40.70	26.08	40.25
2001	1027.00s					

Sources: Labour Bureau: Agricultural labour in India, pp. 158-159.

Socio-Economic Condition of Agricultural Labourer

It is gripping to the note that vast segments of the agricultural labourer are living miserably under geostationary stage. Both for better health, education, housing, habitation, clothing etc are a distant dream. Despite of several five year plans lunched, neither the agricultural sector nor the condition of agricultural labour have been improved. They reacted by a series of factors, likemass illiteracy, poverty, big size family, low level of income, seasonal employment etc are perversions so far the socio-economic condition of agricultural labourers concerned, it is pertinent to discuss the following factors:

(i) Wage structure

(ii) Education

(iii) Housing

(iv) Food

(v) Heath

Wage Structure

Wage is the prime indicates of the labourers for changing their living style of all the problems that face the labourer, that of wages is the most pressing and persistent. Wage is lone of the important incentive which influences the labour supply in numerous productive activities. Since, wage is the only source of income purchasing of food, health care, education, and other social risk are fullfilled. In case of agricultural labourer their average income is derived from wage and employment. Thus, the living condition of agricultural labourers depends on wage rate. Wages of agricultural labourers depends on condition like climate, output, rainfall, demand and supply during the time of harvesting and showing period. During the employment period it is difficult task for fixing the hour of normal working day in agriculture operation with measuring the value of wage rate which are paid by kind. They are always received lower real wage because of non-existence of labour market, non-adequate labour organisation among them self in agrarian sector. The agricultural labourers always acquainted with misery.

Even after the launching of different five year plans the socio-economic status of agricultural persistency classes is far from physiological expectations. It is lamentable to note that the wage structure in agrarian society is fully rigid rather than flexibilities a this is because of the following reasons:

(i) Like the industrial sector there is no strong trade union, association to protect the vast interest of the agricultural labourers.

(ii) A large segment of agricultural labourer are seasonal employed in a year. They don't get full time work rather they work only stipulated time period.

(iii) Majorities of agricultural labourer are unskilled, they don't possess adequate training facilities, specifies educational qualification. And knowledge on modern technology.

(iv) Most of the agricultural labourers are poverty hidden this compels them to work on subsistence wage rates.

(v) Since the agricultural sector does not provides alternative job avenues. Then the agricultural labourers are highly consented on agricultural sector.

To give a moral boost and economic justice the Government has adopted the Minimum Wage Act policy in 1945. The basic objectives of the Minimum Wage Act are not only to support of the subsistence wage but also it is to provide education, medical requirement and amenities. But this policy is totally inapplicable in case of agricultural labourers because they totally unknown about the method to protect their demand by the strong union.

Education

Education enriches and expands the mental and physical development of people but unfortunately the impact of education has not been percolated to the agricultural families. Hence, majority of the agricultural families are illiterate. An account of their literacy they deny their children to attend the school, because they will employ, them in their farm, thus they deprived from the primary education, the dropout rate of school children is very high An account of following reasons:

(i) Illiterate and ignorant parents

(ii) Poverty/economic problems

(iii) Non-stimulating social environment

(iv) Early marriage

(v) Discouraging school environment

Low level of literacy make them educationally backward, consequently they don't par with other labourers due to lack of education. The various programmes, policies lunched by the Government and other agency hamper for implementation in proper manner. They are ignorant about modern technology, high yield seeds, using pesticides, multi-cropping, export qualities of food-grains, self employment etc. Due to this they are unaware about the health hazards, malnutrition, environmental degradation, with standard of living, they purely unknown about the marketing system for selling their product in correct rate, they always smuggling and cheating by the trading person.

Housing

Housing is the primary need of human being in civilized life. It constitutes the most important part of the physical environment, which continuously influences the health and well being of a person. Housing means the provision of comfortable shelter and such surrounding and services as would keep the labourer fit and cheerful for the days of the year.

Out of the basic amenities of life shelter is one among them. The shelter should have minimum four walls with a roof, which is called, as house. It is pre-requisites for taking shelter to protect properties from theft and losses, sunshine, vain, natural calamities, animals and to protect the health hazards, diseases, fungicides and fumes, dust and dirt, and to avoid out side from families securities.

In India majority of families are Agricultural labour class who are living in rural area in a cottage having paddy straw roof with muddy walls and floor which is called kachha house. In this kachha house there are no proper housing facilities. These houses are afraid of disasters like cyclone, flood, fire and other accidents. Every year repairs are required for more than four times, now-a-days the expenses incurred in this house are high if we added the cost incurred as expenses that is more high than the expenses required for a puce house. But, the agricultural labourer unable to construct puce house due to lack of funds. They are also indebted for their farms. So, they again can't collect debts for construction of their house. Their housing condition have thus, been much deplorable and consequently their production is uncertain, so they have no hope of financial sufficient for living in muddy kachha house with one or two room, with accommodate 4 to 5 persons. Due to lack of ventilation and fungus, they are suffering with bronchitis, cough, fever, tuberculosis, and other health hazardous diseases. There is neither safety of house properties nor family securities.

Housing accommodation is not so conducive rather it is an unhygienic. The economic parameters which have included in several Government scheme such as Indira Awas Yojana, Food for work etc are excluded in implementation process for the agricultural labourers classes than than to other sectors. In agricultural sector the basic facilities for housing accommodation, water supply, lighting, toilet, draining are absent. Therefore, housing accommodation is disincentives and more deplorable in agrarian society. Till today lunching the Tenth Five Year Plan no single steps has been included in five year pertaining to the housing accommodation for agricultural labourers.

Fooding

Good calories food always helps for mankind lives standardization with comfortable life. Although the agricultural labourers contributing thousands tonnes of food production for feeding the millions mouth at the sametime they have nothing available for their self-substance, out of their own production they use the some items for their self consumption. The following Table—10.2 reflected about the comparison based if necessary of good calories food for a person with consumption capacities of agricultural labour per day meal.

The Table—10.2 reveals that the family member of agrarian society always consumed less calories with a shortage quantity of food items, intake of food hamper. Their energy, efficiency and integrity. This hampers their vigorous health and doesn't promote robust body. This generates malnutrition problem.

Table 10.2: Consumption capacity of agricultural families in per meals

(in Grams)

Good calories of foods			*Foods or Agricultural families*					
			Children (Categories)			*Adult (Categories)*		
Items	*Children*	*Adults*	*Middle*	*Low*	*Worse*	*Middle*	*Low*	*Worse*
Rice	150 Gms	250 Gms	100 Gms	80 Gms	60 Gms	200 Gms	150 Gms	100 Gms
Wheat	150 Gms	250 Gms	–	–	–	–	–	–
Dal	50 Gms	100 Gms	–	–	–	–	–	–
Sugar	50 Gms	100 Gms	–	–	–	–	–	–
Fresh Fruits	50 Gms	150 Gms	–	–	–	–	–	–
Fresh Vegetable	100 Gms	150 Gms	–	–	–	–	–	–
Other Vegetable	75 Gms	150 Gms	50 Gms	15 Gms	5 Gms	75 Gms	50 Gms	30 Gms
Edible Oil	35 Gms	100 Gms	5 Gms	2 Gms	–	15 Gms	10 Gms	–
Fish/Meat	30 Gms	150 Gms	–	–	–	–	–	–
Egg	1 Pic	2 pic	–	–	–	–	–	–

Source: Compiled from questionnaire.

Food and Nutrition is always helps for better standard of living for every human being but to find about the nutrition requirements of children up to 12 years is not so sufficient in a agrarian society. The intake of nutritions by children in different age group is given the Table—10.3.

Due to lack of balanced diet and consuming unhygienic food they suffer from food allergic, food poison with suffering diseases like cough, cholera, night blind jaundice, fever, dysentery, diarrhoea, respiratory diseases etc. Sometimes they face death, these problems are not admitted to them as their problems, and they are thinking blind beliefs as gunigaride because of unknown about the food scarcity problems.

Health

Agriculture is such culture there is no leisure and pleasure, in this manner agricultural labour endeavour their laborious power for feeding to million starvation and hungry people, but to find about the health condition of family of agricultural labour are very marsh than the other sector labourer. In every organised sector there must be settle medic area facilities to their labourer, their own dispensary with the medical staff ready for give, treatment facilities to their labourer as well as their family members. But in case of agrarian sector there is no separate unit of dispensary activists for health care facilities to them, primary level treatment is better for them with the natural Medicare items. In the organised sector all types of health care facilities are given by the authorities to their labourer like medical advance, medical allowance, sick leave facilities etc. But in case of agricultural laboured these facilities are dream for them. In this manner it is clearly remarks that the health condition of agrarian society is very bad.

Health is a matter of basic self-care with the psychological, mental as well as physical rest is necessary, ill health no longer seen as an unexplained evil, which needs professional magical remedies to cure. But agrarian families self-care are always unrest physical as well as mental rest is not applicable for them. So the families are survivable with suffering great diseases with incurable method, they die with easily preventable disease in the general health status like crude death rate. Infant mortality, life expectancy, prevention and

Table 10.3: Average intake of nutrients according to age and sex

Age Group	Sex	Protein	Fats	Energy	Calcium	IRON	Thiamin	Ribof Lavin	Niacin	Vit-C	Vit-A
		(gms)	(gms)	(Kcal)	(Mg)	(Mg)	(Mg)	(Mg)	(Mg)	(Mg)	(Mg)
1-3	Boys	30.1	16.3	918.1	414.5	8.9	0.69	0.50	7.4	28.5	195.5
	Girls	30.5	15.6	925.9	395.0	9.2	0.70	0.50	7.9	30.1	200.8
4-6	Boys	40.6	20.3	1299.5	432.9	13.0	1.03	0.62	11.1	37.4	249.8
	Girls	41.2	19.1	1298.5	439.6	11.3	1.03	0.63	11.3	38.9	240.7
7-9	Boys	50.0	21.6	1570.3	468.2	20.0	1.37	0.72	13.5	41.5	258.4
	Girls	49.7	23.5	1520.0	472.1	18.3	1.12	0.80	15.8	43.3	246.5
10-12	Boys	56.8	24.9	1847.0	521.9	18.7	1.52	0.83	16.2	50.0	306.6
	Girls	45.7	20.3	1482.2	425.9	15.1	1.23	0.68	13.0	39.6	309.8
13-15	Boys	67.1	28.8	2184.9	612.4	22.1	1.82	1.00	19.6	57.4	356.3
	Girls	65.6	28.4	2097.1	615.4	21.4	1.71	0.98	18.7	60.1	369.4

Source: Ministry of Human Resources Development, Dept. of Women and Chid Development, Govt. of India, Food and Nutrition Board, India Nutrition Profile. p.14-15. 1998

control of communicable diseases, environmental sanitation, maternal and childcare are the hidden way indicators in the agrarian society. Besides this a series of orthodoxies dogmatic fanaticism method such enchanting mantras, offering slaughter mammal and birds to goddesses to avoid the saviours diseases like cholera, typhoid mnemonic, chicken pox and other diseases.

Conclusion

From the above discrimination it is revealed that the social economic condition of agricultural labourer area pitiable and insure mountable camper to the other sector of labour. They spent their rest of life with bereavement, poverty and penuries. Their innocent agony is inevitable forever. They are suppressed and oppressed, exploited and Detroiter by the biog all and lords, middleman and numerous agency. Till end of the 21st century the plight condition of the agricultural labourer have not been mitigated. They born in agriculture, live in agriculture and died in agriculture with indebtedness in this consequence they don't provides basic requirement of life to the members of such big families. In this situation child labour is must. Most of the child labourer are in domestic work with agriculture field, which will be impediment for economic progress in agrarian society.

11

Few Burning Problems of Population in India

R.L. Panigrahy
L.N. Panda

Introduction

India is 2 times of Soviet Union and USA, 5.5 times of Australia, 8 times of Japan, England and France, 12 times of Germany. Out of six people one is from India, it means Indian population is one-sixth of world population. In India each minutes gives birth of 29 new-born babies, in an hour 1740, in a day 41760, in a month 1252800, in a year 15242400 added to the Indian population which is the total population of Australia. India consists of 16.6 crore hector land out of which 14.1 core hector is arable for agriculture. On 100 acres of agriculture land 130 are depended but in Australia it is 27 per cent in France, it is 89 per cent. Hence in India per head agriculture land is 0.35 acre.

Two scientists, Alrik and Fremlik in their book "*The Population Bomb*", stated that such a rate of growth of population occurs in a century. 100 people should live in a gauge of land and in the world 1000 buildings should be constructed, otherwise no roof to live.

Population and Environment

The environmentalists pointed out that up to 33 per cent of land can be utilised for building and establishments. Now, India has been utilising 11 per cent of land for residential establishments. By Govt. record pointed out that 15 to 20 per cent Indian not getting pure drinking water. In spite of 30 croers hector ground water harvesting in rainy season, 40 crores hector ground water utilised by Indian every year. Rapid growth of population became the main factor of environmental pollution by utilising natural resources, misutilisation and mismanagement of utilising natural and manmade resources, discharging chemical substance, industrial influents, petroleum wastes to earth, mass depletion of forests and cutting of trees, insufficient plantation, mass-utilisation of polythenes, bio-diversity, etc are the major factors of population of air, water, earth which causes mental pollution of Indian people. It causes health hazard of not only people live in but also other habitats on the earth. Trees are the agents to make the environment clean and to live the living organs on the earth safely. Due to mass depletion of forest the air, earth, water can not be purified, soil erosion increases, monsoon disorder and disaster occurs, disorder of ozone layer happens, temperature of air increases. Air pollution and increase in temperature and decrease of oxygen content in it make holes in ozone layer. It passes sun ray to earth directly, that is hazardous to the living organs on the earth. Due to these cases the ice mountains of the cold countries are starting to be liquefied, which will increase the water level of sea 7 meters in coming 100 years. It became an alarming danger to the globe. Air and noise pollution became a common factor of people's daily life due to increasing population and use of vehicles, industries and allied services in the day-to-day livelihood. It occurs metal disorder and madness especially in young generation. This also occurs many new diseases which can be identified by the medical personnel.

Population and Health

HIV/AIDS became a danger in the society. It is more in Less Developed Countries (LDCs). In LDCs most people are uneducated and illiterate. So, they are less aware of HIV/AIDS. Sharing of sex became an amusement to the lower class and downtrodden people those who are mainly illiterate. Due to their ignorance they think it as an epidemic disease. So, they can not understand what is HIV/AIDS? How it is transmitted? How to behave with HIV/AIDS infected people ? What are its remedial measures? People always thought about why Govt. has not produced any medicine to prevent/cure it. The answer of these questions can be to educated these people by mass education.

Govt. and the health educators, NGOs has been educating the public through awareness campaign and IEC materials to know about HIV/AIDS patients that the weight and height of the person will be lower down day-by-day, the colour of the body will be pale, sides of the eye will be black, continuous suffering of fever and dysentery, indigestion, etc. Now-a-days many diseases have same symptoms found out after all she is not affected with HIV/AIDS. Since, 2/3 years Govt. of India has a movement to remove TB from the country under DOTS (Direct Observation of Treatment Service) with the assistance of Denmark Govt. known as DANTB. DOTS has medicines duly distribute by the PHCs through Anganwadi workers, NGO people, Village Health Workers, volunteers as DOTS provide to cure TB patients. In spite of death effected with HIV/AIDS, relatives telling that the patient was affected by TB. TB is not shy, but AIDS is a social stigma. In rural areas people heard about AIDS, but they don't know who and why AIDS affects. They don't know about safe sex. No body can understand them about the same, because sex is secret. It is quite personal and a delicate subject. Sex is an open secret. Day-by-day sex became an enjoyment among teen-aged people, the lower class and downtrodden people. The environmental pollution, massive use of fertilisers and pesticides in firm, exposure of chemical and petroleum products, heavy industrialisation, depletion of forest, unconsciousness of people on environment, viewing of modern fashionable programmes on television and movies, etc. make the people more sexually attracted. More consumption of drugs, intoxicants, liquor, non-vegetable food articles, etc. make the internal body and mind weaker only increases evil sentiments and sexual attitudes. For poor communities, backward castes, daily labourers in construction sector, people living in slum areas, pavements and railway sides, etc. are not in the covered of Indian population census and/or not the beneficiaries of Govt. programmes/policies. Their only entertainment is viewing cinema, drinking alcohol and intoxicants, enjoying sex in family, relatives and for earning. They are interested to produce more children which will feed the parents in the old age and in day-to-day life also. In lighting the social people hatred them and in dark they enjoy them for sexual amusements by paying something. These women also moving at road sides of long line roads and NH sides. The drivers and staff working in transporting vehicles are away from their residences from days long, so they take the sex relation with them. The college going girls also doing this in seeking lift to the trucks and transporting vehicles on the highways. The Dhabas (roadside overnight hotels) are also engaging them for sex at night. Adolescents and college going girls are also earning by moving to nearby other towns in the name of study. They are also engaging themselves in the big hotels and restaurants for sex and earning which meets their day-to-day expenses in western fashionable manner. These college going girls also supplying their friends and relative girls for the same trade by motivating them as amusement and earning. These ladies are spreading HIV/AIDS, TB, Hepatitis, etc. In metros the cost of living became high, the parents can not fulfil all the requirements of the children with the steps of the changing society, so sex is a very good secret business to earn without investment, pain, loss. They are enjoying both the financial and sexual benefits. Sometimes, it occurs rape, kidnapping, murder, love harassment, sex abuses, etc. Adolescents going to the hotels, lodges which gives scope to kidnap them. As employment problem prevailed mostly in India like countries, women are interested to empower themselves by earning something through service sector. Many people taking its chance to migrate them from one place to other. In rural and semi-urban areas the women labourers are the sex workers at evening time while returning to home after work completed. This is over time (OT) in their concept. By their concept sharing of sex has no expenses or loss, but a windfall gain. By labour how much they can earn? In a day work with hardship they can earn 50 to 100 rupees. But in few minutes of sharing sex they can earn more than expectations. So, they are sharing sex at evening after work otherwise their family members may ask or they can be blamed socially or they can be legally picked up. Few college going adolescents are encouraging their class mates and other relatives to amuse sex and also supplying them to the sex customers, hotels, restaurants, brokers earning money. Not only this they are also addicting drug consumption and drug abuses to the college going students. The rural youth are migrating to distant industrial and urban places for their livelihood. As they are away from their family they are making sex with the local sex workers. In these cases, the HIV occurs and found out as AIDS patient which make the secrets done by them open to the public as an affect which can not be kept secret and has no remedy. In developed countries sex is free and an aristocracy. In less developed countries it is in such positions. From the HIV/AIDS infected patients 95 per cent of them are in less developed countries. No doubt this disease is transmitted from developed countries. 4 per cent of affected people are due to transmission of virus through infected syringes and 7 per cent by the syringe taken drugs, other are by unsafe sex. One fourth of total AIDS patients are women. Women are infected with HIV fastly than male. They are AIDS driven. Due to this few children in womb are AIDS infected. The incidence of mother-to-child (vertical) transmission has accounted for more than 90 per cent of all HIV infected worldwide are infants and children. In sub-Saharan countries one among five over aged people infected with HIV/AIDS. As an "AIDS Epidemics update 2003" 30 lakh AIDS patient died and 30 lakh living. In last 1992-2002 years, American AIDS patients increased five times surveyed by Centre for Disease Control & Prevention. By December 2003, the diseased AIDS patients are 30 lakhs and infected are 50 lakhs and infected are 30 lakhs. UNICEF studied by 2015 AIDS orphan expected to hit 25 million. India, China, Rusia, Nigeria, Ethiopia are the five countries, by 2010 will be 50 to 75 million AIDS patients. US National Intelligence Council studied India is likely to have 20 to 25 million AIDS patients. In a survey by Durex, a contraceptive company (out of 49 states with 50 thousand people surveyed) France people making sex relation for 167 time, Singapore people for 110 times, British people for 149 times, Thailand people for 112 times, American people for 139 times, whereas Indian are lowest in this aspect. 50 per cent of France lovers and 30 per cent partners have HIV positive in their body. Out of 10 people in India, 4 are unaware of sexual relations before marriage. But it is an alarming danger that 26 per cent Indian, 61 per cent Sweden do not use condom at the time of their intercourse.

In developing countries like India Infant Mortality Rate (IMR) is very high. The picture of IMR of India is shown in the following table as per Govt. record. In spite of this, many are not under the Govt. record who have not registered in any medical.

Estimated Infant Mortality Rate (IMR) by Rural-Urban States, 2000

India/States/	*Total*	*Rural*	*Urban*
1	*2*	*3*	*4*
Andhra Pradesh	65	74	36
Assam	75	78	35
Bihar	62	63	53
Gujarat	62	69	45
Haryana	67	69	57
Karnataka	57	68	24
Kerala	14	14	14
Madhya Pradesh	88	94	54
Maharashtra	48	57	33
Orissa	96	99	66
Punjab	52	56	38
Rajasthan	79	83	58
Tamil Nadu	51	57	38
Uttar Pradesh	83	87	65
West Bengal	51	54	37
Arunachal Pradesh	44	45	11
Chhatisgarh	79	95	49
Delhi	32	32	32
Goa	23	24	21
Jharkhand	70	74	48
Himachal Pradesh	60	62	37
Jammu & Kashmir	50	51	45
Manipur	23	23	25
Meghalaya	58	61	32
Mizoram	21	24	15

(Contd...)

1	2	3	4
Nagaland	NA	NA	23
Sikkim	49	49	36
Tripura	41	42	32
Uttranchal	50	73	26
Union Territories			
Andaman & Nicobar	23	27	10
Chandigarh	28	38	26
Dadra & Nagar Haveil	58	62	14
Daman & Diu	48	38	57
Lakshadweep	27	25	29
Pondicherry	23	33	15
India	**68**	**74**	**43**

Source: India Registrar General, Vital Statistics Division. (2001). Sample Registration System Bulletin, October 2001, New Delhi. P. 1.

Women's Studies

Society is not homogeneous. Societal classification may be of different kinds, are such in gender. Gender discrimination is major topic in LDCs, in developed country it is more prevalent, but that is less concerned because developed countries are matriarchal in nature, women are more empowered than man. But in almost all countries women have a lower development status as compared to men. Hence, there is a need of paradigm shift. There are the problems of gender discrimination as a result of infant and child mortality, intensively affected malnutrition to girl child, amniocentesis and female foeticide, sex ratio in general and juvenile, missing women, food availability and health care, education, work participation, etc. In this consequences women have taken many advanced steps as compared to men and are trying to be equal and sometimes more than men. Every Govt. is encouraging them through many policy measures and protecting them from evil and hazards with legal frameworks. So, India Govt. had made 33 per cent reservation and empowering them more with incoming amendments of the Indian Constitution. The inequalities of women are in such a juncture that they live in a glass house. According to a new research from the University of Exeter England, women at the top ladder are being promoted into risky and precarious leadership positions, where the chances of failure is high. If everything spirals downwards, they get the blame. They may find themselves up against yet another invisible barrier, so-called as "glass cliff". In an article in *London Times* last year, women are blamed in their jobs as "weaker havoc" as compared to men. So any business world be better of without women. Psychologists Michelle Ryan and Alex Haslam were convinced that corporate failure is the fault of women, which causes negative outcome. British Journal of Management found women carrying high risk of failure. Dr. Ryan and Prof. Haslam pointed out that the organisations that had been doing badly appointing women into the leadership role, their performance is placed under close scrutiny. Women in such position are highly visible and hence come under much more attack than a men in similar situation. They suggested that women cannot be out of sexism. Ms. Worman feels that high calibre women will go off and set up on their own rather than attempt to fit into an inflexible organisation.

REFERENCES

1. Crude Results of Population Explosions, *Dainik Asha* (Oriya Daily), 18.06.2000.
2. *Samaya*, Oriya Daily, 30.10.2004.
3. Andrea Wren, Risk of Women At the Top, *The Hindu*-Vsakhapatanam, 14th Sept' 2004.
4. Chaudhury, Aninadm, Mass Illiteracy and the Mafia Raj, *The Statesman*, Bhubaneswar, 3rd November' 2004.
5. Prof. Guha, Jaba, *Synopsis on Development & Gender*, Jadavpur University, Kolkata.
6. Boys Beware of Girls, *The Samaj* (Oriya Daily), 3.11.2004.
7. Statistics Reference Annual, Ministry of Statistics, Govt. of India.

Index

R

S